Contemporary Asian Australian Poets

Contemporary Asian Australian Poets

Edited by

Adam Aitken, Kim Cheng Boey
& Michelle Cahill

PUNCHER & WATTMANN

© 2013

First published in 2013

Published by Puncher and Wattmann
PO Box 441
Glebe NSW 2037

http://www.puncherandwattmann.com

puncherandwattmann@bigpond.com

National Library of Australia
Cataloguing-in-Publication entry:

Aitken, Adam, Boey, Kim Cheng & Cahill, Michelle

Contemporary Asian Australian Poets
ISBN   9781921450655 (paperback)
        9781922186317 (ebook)
        9781922186324 (kindle)

I. Title.

A821.3

Cover design by Matthew Holt

Printed by McPhersons Printing Group

This project has been assisted by the Australian Government through the Australia Council, its arts funding and advisory body.

Australian Government

Australia Council
for the Arts

Contents

Preface

In the early stages of planning the anthology, we were inclined towards a thematic structure as a coherent framework to represent the poets gathered here – poets who are either first-generation migrants from Asia or Australia-born poets who can trace their roots to Asia. In the two years since the first seed of the project was planted, we have discarded the thematic approach in favour of a looser, alphabetical arrangement. This shift came about principally due to the diversity of poetry and poets we have met along the way. There are of course the obviously Asian poets whose works are centred on migration and meditations of home and belonging. But there are many Asia-born poets and those of Asian descent who do not fit the neat categories we started out with, who refuse or contest the category of "Asian Australian" or even "Asian" or "Australian," poets who have chosen more postmodern and theory-oriented paths, eschewing identity narrative and politics.

There were other structural layouts we considered: country of origin or ancestry, generation and chronology. But these divisions seemed contrived and distract from shared concerns and poetics, creating artificial boundaries where there is fluidity and dialogic interaction among the poets and poems. In considering the geopolitical approach, we were led to deeper questions of the extent and boundaries of Asia, and what it means to be Asian. There are poets like Nora Krouk, of Russian heritage but born in Harbin, China, and also poets from the periphery of Asia, Iran-born Ali Alizadeh and many others. In the end we decided to draw the boundaries closer, in part due to space constraint, and mostly due to coherence and focus. We also omitted Asian Australians writing in their native tongue; though some if it has been translated, it would blow the project open to unwieldy proportions. It is our hope that our effort will lead the way for further exposure to what we think is a rich but neglected part of Australian literature.

While in the United States, there has already been a host of anthologies featuring American poets of Asian origin or descent, there has been no single collection focussing on Asian Australian writers. Our belief in the importance of the project, and the diverse excellence of the poets we have curated, have sustained us over the last two years, despite being such different poets. Each poet here represents an intersection of two or more cultures and languages, and their works constitute a poetry that is in conversation with the parallel poetries that are changing the landscape of Australian literature. We have tried to be inclusive and thorough but there are a few enforced omissions due to irresolvable difficulties.

We would like to express our gratitude to our contributors; they have been patient and unstinting in offering their work. We would like to thank David Musgrave for taking on the project, and to writers, friends and family who have given us support and encouragement.

Three Perspectives

What does "Asian Australian" sound like, and what does that sound say about ethnicity and identity in Australia today? Beyond the obvious fact of English being our lingua franca, there is a fascinating range of "dialects" in relation to the poetry collected here. Take Omar Musa's western suburbs teenager in 'Airforce Ones' raving about a new brand of Nikes:

> LUCKY for me, I just got paid. I count it out:
> 1, 2, 3, 4, 5, 6 fifties.
> That's three hundred bucks.
> So I break my bread, so I shave my head, so I'm ready to go

With a contemporary tone, such a voice moves beyond the confessional lyric or the iambic mini-autobiography one finds in much mainstream poetry nowadays. This kind of Australian rap-inspired English hardly speaks to a unifying poetic, or even a theory of how to write. In a sense Musa's consumer Asian Aussie speaks as a subject already dis-engaged from debates about race and identity. He is post-identity. Brian Castro remarks that language enables a shedding of the identity, or enables enactments of alternatives: 'Language marks the spot where the self loses its prison bars – where the border crossing takes place, traversing the spaces of others.' (1)

The term Asian Australian may sound exotic or merely ironic and self-deprecating. We may use it to self-orientalise and to be performative. Asian Australians are chameleons or ventriloquists and take on a diversity of positions, or engage a striking range of moods, attitudes and modalities. Even as we attempt to define our focus by deploying the category of *Asian* , the poets here offer choice: to speak as an authentic member of a minority culture and to be strategically essentialist, or to use the resources to speak doubly, to hybridise oneself, to reveal or to hide, to wear disguise, to ironise and parody onself and others. The choices are there in the very constructed nature of displaced writing, in which difference proliferates beyond clichés.

Asian Australian poetry engages a cosmopolitanism and a sense of worldliness that is a product of our multiculturalism, but it is also something more. Such poetry debates are seemingly incommensurable categories that structure so much discourse about migrants: race, difference, assimilation or resistance. Many of these poets are chroniclers of the arrivant experience. Others offer celebratory discourses. Some of the poems explore migrant autobiography, some poems invoke an Asian childhood, which is often nurturing and warm and nostalgic, though there are also poems that ironise this, as if the poem about heritage had become a genre that needed critique.

So this collection does more that celebrate the multicultural melting pot in Australia. Some poets draw attention to cosmopolitan multiculturalism's cool "disinterestedness". Ouyang Yu, for example, often parodies this profit-loss equation of being a fragmented Chinese Aussie who can't fit in; rather than assure the host-foster "parent", and rejecting a conciliatory tone Yu holds a provocative mirror up to Australia, which he often figures as a rather paternalistic host. Yu's ornate and ironic dramatic monologues function to antagonise assimilationists.

Other voices of resistance favour a more confessionary approach. Some poets define themselves as members of families which hope to maintain ancient Asian traditions. This journey back to parental origins is a positive, though other poems express disappointment at the loss of connection, as if a condition of living in Australia was the requirement to abandon or forget so much of one's first language and culture.

Asian Australian poets approach this crucial entanglement with exile in varied ways. Ee Tiang Hong declares a Yeatsian ambivalence about the plight of races in postcolonial Malaysia. For Sudesh Mishra Fiji's postcolonial history and subsequent reification of Fijian Melanesian identity over Indian migrant identity is a complex and emotively *public* subject and a mode of postcolonial critique that requires a certain public style of poem. For some Vietnamese Australian poets, the Vietnam War and its aftermath has not ceased to matter as a topic that addresses their own unique deracination. A similar experience animates the poems of Sunil Govinnage and Desh Balasubramaniam, both Sri Lankan migrants.

Eileen Chong's poems of her ancestry describe complex movements between her Australian home and the different reference sites for her Straits Chinese identity (Singapore, Hong Kong, Malaysia). Chong is affectionate and ironic, absolutely aware that the return to roots risks becoming a semi-touristic indulgence. For Jessie Tu writing about her uncle's return from Taiwan to China, it is the homeland that denies redemption ('House'). For Merlinda Bobis, home is not merely an empirical space but an Imaginary in which the dramatic lyric debates colonialism, migration (in terms of a movement from rural to urban spaces, and between East and West) and the sexual dynamic of the colonised female and her relation to the colonising male. Her Philippines and its story is mythological and circular, and for her, there is a sense of who and where she is located; there is no inside/outside to structure the poem. Her poems seem both located rhizomically in the Philippines and outside of it and can be read as multimodal texts for theatrical performance.

It is a fascinating fact that while much of the subject matter of these poems refers to non-Anglo worlds, this anthology is made in the English language and contains poetry that inherits canonical forms and functions of English verse culture, like the ode, the satire, the elegy (Ee Tiang Hong, and Mishra) as well as the traditions of modernist poetics that are familiar to many followers of poetry in this country today. In Debbie Lim's animal poems we can find a Taoist or Zen aesthetic married to a tradition of modern American ecopoetics. Michelle Cahill's feminist and postcolonial poems occupy a Hindu-Buddhist conceptual space that is also highly crafted to deliver a deep feminist critique (influenced by Spivak among others) of the feminine subaltern, and an awareness of how the East continues to be orientalised in (and in turn de-stabilise) Western thinking.

Destabilising the primacy of English, Bobis uses indigenous Bikol, Pilipino, and Tagalog phrases alongside the English. James Stuart (a clearly post-identitarian poet) is also highly language aware and attuned to how identity is very much embedded in globalisation and mass media: 'For hours I would channel surf a TV that had been turned / upside down & emptied of intelligible signs' (the white horse). In Bella Li's texts a subtle political act of disobedience is enacted by a Chinese student/intellectual lawyer who knows about East-West antagonisms and the power of grand narratives. She chooses to treat "China" as an unstable term, a geo-spatial referent for Chinese imperial history, which functions as a mythic foundation for the authority of the current Communist oligarchy. Her poems are more like deracinated explorer journals than elegies *à la recherche du temps perdu*. China is not hers, and it is not anyone's, not even an Emperor's. China is a library.

Younger emerging poets like Christine Ratnasingham, a Sri Lankan raised in England and in Australia, remind us that however much we want to imagine ourselves as raceless, colourless citizens of a multicultural paradise, skin colour still limits our choice of being who we want to be:

> I forget I have it, until I remember my childhood
> when nearly every student felt they needed
> to remind me that I was not of their whiteness
>
> I forget it clothes me, until I leave home
> (From 'Dark Skin')

Embedded in transnational connections, the Asian-Australian is no more certain of self definition than any other kind of Australian. But such uncertainty is creative. These poets modulated their Asianness through various imaginary scenarios, and a multiplicity of Asias emerges. In Nguyễn Tiên Hoàng's poems about Vietnam, which he left after the end of the war, Vietnam is not that topos found in popular Australian cookery books and travel shows. Returning there, it is hardly recognisable to the poet himself, except as the ever changing node of place, nation, and identity, which is the salient point of his work: that the concept of "the Vietnamese" is a contestable category. When juxtaposed to poems about suburban Canberra or Melbourne, his poems (and Vuong Pham's) re-iterate the dilemma of the diasporic Vietnamese identity in the West, the "dilemma" as a subject for creative recollection, lyrical meditation, and a mode of political critique.

On the other hand Ivy Alvarez (a highly published *international* poet) gives the impression that she writes wherever she is at the time, and that the potential reader could be Mexican or Irish. Miriam Lo, a Chinese Australian based in Perth, writes feminist critiques of the sexism inherent in the Confucian impact of her heritage. Her grandmother poem (one of a many in this book) is both an affirmation of roots as well as a critique of male sexism. Lo deploys her sameness-in-difference to spotlight misogyny affecting the lives of migrant mothers in Australia, who must endure the double-edged sword of filial duty and being a good modern, suburban housewife.

If identity politics is a part of community politics, the Asian Australian artist may happily fulfil a role as model migrant and a native informant on topics such as Buddhism, food connoisseurship, tea drinking, and quiet temple worship and other exemplary activities that promise harmony. On the other hand others are destabilised by antagonistic or ambivalent feelings and are more explicit about breaking community taboos. Canadian-Chinese-Australian Andy Quan describes how the very site of the Asian queer body is both a site of various disciplinary frames as well as the zone of pleasure, part and parcel of diverse networking of queer as well as straight community. Quan writes to find connections and moments of solidarity which are often sited in childhood scenes, at school, and in iconic queer places like saunas. All this add up to a complex identity that invites endless re-iteration and re-configuration. Quan's lyric unites these disparities.

Here then are poems about the shocking impact of being othered; for example, Paul Dawson's 'Thanks for the Poems Pauline Hanson'. But there is no set temperature in this anthology. There is a continuum from the cool, phlegmatic commentary on Australian suburbia to the much more angry and indignant protest poem. Between these extremes are lyrics of varying calm.

Once the 'basic' identity of the poet is declared other issues can be explored, and even the very premise of origin and inheritance through family connection is worth contesting. These poems will raise questions about the way a previously absent Asian heritage becomes a presence. As Jaya Savige shows in 'Currency Lad', a sense of a national identity emerges unexpectedly and in an unplanned, almost delinquent way. Savige's currency lad (child of convict and migrants) is not an orphan without a future, and does not *suffer* disconnection with mother England, but is the exemplar of how the hybrid allows a new connection through difference. Savige's poems suggest that the disconnection of place from nationality, even if it was mired in violence and suffering, allows a vital regrowth to occur. The various points of origin, however, are indeed worth preserving and celebrating.

ADAM AITKEN

Notes

(1) Brian Castro, "Writing Asia", in *Looking For Estrellita*, p 152, St Lucia: UQP, 1999.

Migration is not a simple act of complete uprooting and swapping one home and culture for another, abandoning one's past life and starting a fresh slate in a new environment. The decision to leave sets in motion a train of consequences that does not cease with the act of transplanting to and entrenchment within a new culture and language; it triggers a continuing process of negotiation, of shuttling back and forth between places, between the past and present, and between lives and narratives. Despite their avowal not to return and their determination to settle in the adoptive home, the impulse among migrant writers to look back is irrepressibly strong. Unlike their second or more generation counterparts, first-generation migrant writers carry with them a heavy freight of ideas and memories, especially if a significant part of their lives has been spent in the original homeland. For better or worse, this burden creates a gravitational pull towards the life and home left behind; the memories of the homeland are lived, and strong, and create binaries of old homeland/adopted home, past/ present, self/other that the writers have to constantly negotiate.

Ee Tiang Hong migrated from Malacca to Perth in 1975, just after Gough Whitlam had abolished the White Australia Policy with his declaration of Australia as 'a multicultural nation, in which linguistic and cultural heritage of the Aboriginal people and of peoples from all parts of the world can find an honoured place.' Escaping the repressive politics that ruled Malaysia in the 60s and 70s, Ee is resolved to make a clean break with the past: 'Sever the cord straight through/ in one brave stroke, and then/ forget, (my mother used to say),/ or else the heart will fray' ('The Burden'). He is determined to establish a new sense of home and self in his adoptive country, but the note of resignation is unmistakable: 'Here, halfway up the Swan, I chose/ to build my house, for the last time,/ having to come to terms with my new home' ('Perth'). However firm his resolve to make a fresh start appears to be, Ee cannot resist making constant imaginary returns to his hometown. His post-migration work is informed by the topos of Malacca, and makes comparative surveys of his place of birth and his adoptive country. But Ee is aware of the pitfalls of nostalgia, cautious of what Salman Rushdie diagnoses as 'some urge to reclaim, to look back, even at the risk of being mutated into pillars of salt' (*Imaginary Homelands* 10). His poems resist the sentimental backward look; they are attempts to yoke disparate locations and cultures together in a new mapping of self and place.

Ee's poems negotiate the complex processes of uprooting and settlement, of negotiating liminal zones, slippery borderlands between places of the past and where he is now. They commute between two geographies, involuntarily, sometimes feverishly, as if by doing so he can resolve the binary tension, reconcile the conflicted sense of belonging, and appease the sense of displacement, of being neither here nor there, where one drifts in 'the space, the silences between' ('Some New Perspectives').

The comparative or bifocal vision that sees one place in terms of another is a reflex among migrants. Moving in the liminal spaces between the adopted home and the place of origin, they seek to discover or create connective threads, networks of social ties and memories that will sponsor a sense of belonging and home, albeit provisional. However, the sense of being in-between, of being neither here nor there, can be overwhelming and in the case of Ouyang Yu, this liminality exacerbates the alienation and displacement that he experiences as a migrant writer seeking to define himself in a dominantly Anglo-Celtic literary environment. His work makes a bold and outspoken stand against assimilation, the personae often disenfranchised Chinese migrants rebuking the token multiculturalism and the perceived racism in Australian culture: 'You expect me to be integrated into the mainstream/ I don't care although I become a citizen/ Not to strengthen your national identity as you like to think' ('The Ungrateful Migrant'). Resisting the pressure on the migrant to assimilate and conform to the culture and language of the Anglo-Celtic majority, Ouyang's work is firmly insistent on difference, on being contrapuntal, suspicious of any essentialist and monolithic view of culture, be it Australian or Chinese. His work captures the doubleness that the migrant feels, moving between two languages and cultures:

> my surname is china
> my given name australia
> if i translate that direct into english
> my surname becomes australia
> my given name china
> i do not know what motherland means
> i possess two countries
> or else
> i possess neither   ('The Double Man')

Ouyang's work is often seen to be vehemently protesting the hypocrisies of Australian society, the voice of his personae often vitriolic, but his work is far more complex than it appears and has over the years shed some of its anger. A key word in understanding his work is "translation"; shuttling between two countries, he is constantly translating across linguistic and cultural borders, and becomes in the process a translated person, a hybridized diasporic subjectivity neither wholly Chinese nor Australian. Ouyang's voice and style are distinctly his, a result of the mongrel diction and rhythms he employs, embodying the process of translation in poems that reflect multiculturalism in action, on the streets, not on the lips of politicians, in suburbs like 'Kingsbury, in the late 1990s' where English is spoken with 'new accents' ('New Accents').

Merlinda Bobis and Miriam Wei Wei Lo also enact this process of translation in their work, embedding their ancestral languages in poems that map the routes and roots of migration. Bobis's poem 'This is where it begins' is threaded through with Tagalog and Spanish, as she weaves the narrative that recovers her heritage and origins in the Philippines. The poem begins with lines of Tagalog before setting the scene of the ancestral home, and embracing Bobis's cultural heritage and roots: 'And so this poem is for my father, mother, grandmother, grandfather and all the storytellers,/ the conjurers who came before us.' The poem is an imaginary return that enables Bobis to maintain and renew ties with her ancestral homeland; more importantly it is an attempt to discover connective threads between the past and present, to find narrative coherence that will align her family history with the continuing story.

In poems that explore her hybrid inheritance, Lo also grafts another language onto the body of English words. In her debut collection *Against Certain Capture*, she delves into the twin aspects of her make-up: her mother's Anglo-Scottish lineage and her father Malaysian Chinese origins. The first half the collection reconstructs the life of her father's mother, Liang Yue Xian, retracing her diasporic route from Canton to Kuching. Into the narrative Lo inserts Chinese script, including Liang's name; the embedding of Chinese characters into the body of the English poem underscores the poet's bicultural heritage, and forges new ways of belonging, attachments and affiliations across linguistic, temporal and spatial boundaries.

In her essay 'Reconstructing Asian-American Poetry: A Case for Ethnopoetics,' Shirley Lim observes how in Asian American poetry the sense of exclusion and marginalization in the hostland, and the fear of 'the loss of identity' that comes with assimilation, generate an ethnopoetics (the deployment of ethnic themes, images, speech) that has the power to subvert monolithic nationalism and enact the complex aspects of Asian American identities. Similarly, in Asian Australian poetry, the ethnopoetic reflex creates motifs and themes revolving around the lost home and culture. In Bobis and Lo it manifests itself in images and memories of familial figures, and inextricably linked with these are the motifs of food, cooking and eating, essential constituents of Asian culture and identity. Lo's 'Mooncake' is triggered by the Chinese mid-autumn festival, the traditional pastry becoming not just an emblem of Chinese heritage, but also disruption with it, and triggers questions of what and where home is. Eileen Chong's 'Mid-Autumn Mooncakes,' prompted by the same occasion, transplants the images and memories of festival and her parents, to Australia, and offers solace to the migrant poet, alone and hungry for familial connections. However, Chong avoids the sentimental pitfalls of nostalgia; the poem circles back to the present that finds an image emblematic of her migrant condition 'My bowl, a cradle of bright congee/ full of the gold of the mid-autumn moon.'

In 'Grandmother's Dish' Chong reconstructs a family recipe, in the process transplanting her culinary inheritance to Australian soil. Like Lo's Chinese grandmother, Chong's is an embodiment of her Chinese heritage, a repository of culinary knowledge that provides is sustaining and affirming; the recitation of her recipe brings comfort to the migrant poet and yields a moment of connection between past and present. The recurrence of culinary motifs in Asian migrant poetry reflects the importance of food and rituals related to it and their connection to the complex processes of remembering. Memory is an alimentary act, ingesting, digesting and assimilating, mediating between what is outside and what is within, between that which is past and the here and now. Shen's 'Noodles,' like the noodles in Chong's 'Winter Meeting,' evokes the poet's ethnic and cultural heritage, but while Chong's poem depicts a moment of communion between two migrants with a common origin, Shen's bowl of noodles confronts him with a part of himself that he seems uneasy with, his Chinese heritage. As a Chinese migrant from Malaysia, his Chineseness is doubly mediated, translated through two acts of migration. Chinese emigrants from South-East Asian countries whose ancestors had emigrated from China to the colonies of the British Empire just a generation or more ago can be considered doubly diasporic. For them the idea of Chineseness is fraught with difficulty. Likewise, for a Fijian Indian Australian like Sudesh Mishra and an Indian Australian like Michelle Cahill, with their hybridised histories and subjectivities, the idea of India and Indianness is not a static myth of ancestral homeland that they can lay claim to, but something they have to negotiate and reinvent.

Home is never a given, for first-generation migrants, and continues to be a complex issue for subsequent generations. Being beneficiaries of two or more cultures, and entangled in complex webs of affiliations and attachments, they are wary of identity politics and monolithic formations. As part of the Asian diaspora they are actively inventing new ways of being Asian and looking at Asia, creating transnational networks that bind Australia to China, India, Thailand, Vietnam, Malaysia, Singapore and other parts of Asia, adding to social heterogeneity in these countries, even as they enrich the multicultural diversity of Australia. In their work there is an ongoing traffic between the here and there, the local, the regional and the global, past and present, their poetic transactions changing the ways in which Asia looks at Australia and enriching Australian imaginings of Asia, offering new insights into what it means to be Asian Australian.

KIM CHENG BOEY

The Female Text

Of the thirty seven poets we have anthologised, seventeen are women. As a group they are collectively more varied than similar in terms of writing styles, cultural background, biographies, tracing their origins from at least ten countries in north, east and south Asia; yet they comprise a vital contribution to Asian Australian poetics. I would go further to claim a pioneering survey by these female poets, compelled as they are by the double exile of migration and mediation of patriarchal terrain, so inimical to the female psyche.

Within cultural spaces language has the power to bind women's material and emotional realities to aesthetic and seemingly apolitical philosophical paradigms, shaped predominantly by men. Back in the 80s the Australian feminist Dale Spender wrote extensively of the man-made language that excludes women and their experience. More recently Devleena Ghosh has written about spaces of counteraction for Asian women in an Australian context. (1) Ania Walwicz has written of how, being placed outside the norms of society, 'both the migrant and the woman are in the same position. They have to deal with conflict...(with) no sense of belonging.' (2)

Looking stereoscopically, forwards and backwards, one is struck by the sophistication and ingenuity by which they have re-imagined their identities in ways that are transnational and to varying extents translational. The similarities in their themes, and the differences in their poetics are evidence that a spectrum of positions, including those allied with feminism or postmodernism can contest cultural representations and patriarchal authority.

Some of these women may be described as activists, engaging discursively, at times self-reflexively to renegotiate the lived experience of exclusion, loss and reinvention, to excavate the silent violence of colonialism. Louise Ho's 'A Veteran Talking' directly addresses the rape and force of the Nanjing massacre: 'We did what had to be done:/Shooting, knifing, hanging, burning,' In 'Dark Skin' Christine Ratnasingham reverses memory to discreetly accentuate a visceral trauma. Ten Ch'in Ü (Maureen Ten) probes with a Daoist questioning of identity and power.

Second or third generation women poets may not feel such acute disturbances yet many are concerned to explore their Asian ancestry, the conditions of entry and departure from country to country. Migration is experienced through a lens of psychic fragility in the figurative lyrics of Jessie Tu. Suneeta Peres da Costa modulates spaces of irony in which violence and estrangement are palpable.

Variations of allegory can mediate complexity. Mona Attamimi's poetic allegories revisit the brutal impact of Dutch imperialism. Like the *balaidera* in my poem 'Ode to Mumbai', Attamimi's Betawi intentionally conflates sexual and colonial tyranny, the one complicating the other. With their abundant temporal clauses and repetitions, Bella Li's prose poems are discontinuous, beautifully rendered and portentous; Attamimi's poems have an alluring simplicity and strength. These narratives never fully disclose, suggesting the arbitrary and provisional nature of the official account, its reliance on the reader over 'oriental historians,'(to quote Li). Allegory foregrounds that history is an act of writing and reading, a discursive practice that can be revised. It questions the fixed status of history, inviting the reader to unmask neo-colonial subtexts that continue to oppress.

Ivy Alvarez writes fragmented and allusive narratives which are performative at the edges, the voids of gender and culture. Drawing on her Filipino-Spanish-Australian-Welsh connections dualisms are gently provoked in poems like 'there's only ever been two'. Alvarez is adept at the partial-image ripe with assonance. Her condensed stanzas seem to shape their own tongue:

> your bones'
> brittle semaphore tattoo
> out how far you fell how much
> we have a third between us
> a shift a shadow drawing
> down the lids in noonday sun
> shuttering hush of lashes
> we say too much with fragile
> instruments supreme Geiger
> counters tick tick tick burr

In her fine poem 'Curing the animal' she voices the emotional despair of a pastoralist's wife, whose task is to skin and cure a wallaby, the animal suggestive of a corresponding carnal encounter.

> He is away all the day in the dust.
> *a eucalypt oil smell taints his neck*
> *he comes to me*
> *bones meeting mine*
> *a hard fit*
> *a green lawn at the edge of a desert*
> *my heart, inexact*
> There is a sharp knife in the house.

It's a far cry from the meditative, animal-themed lyrics of Australian-born Debbie Lim. Lim's precise imagism derives from a tradition of Western aesthetics: there's the distinct influence of Rilke and Judith Beveridge. Even still, a curbed wrath is evident in 'Bamboo' and 'How to Grow Feet of the Golden Lotus.' In Carol Chan's open-ended stanzas, the civic and the personal resonate with a trace of her trans-Pacific movements:

> Are we on the same side of the question,
> or are you tracing a common state
> meant for no-one but the future you think is possible,
> the one I do not see.

Of the younger migrant poets the Pakistani writer/musician, Misbah Khokhar, makes an arresting protest against male violence in prose poems from her sequence *Rooftops in Karachi*. There is an edgy verve here as material objects give way to insight, a refreshing demystification of Islam in 'Possession', a liberation of memory and border politics in poems like 'Veils as Flags'

> The solution is to dispense with lines. Someone must rub out the demarcation lines that have been painted over valleys and mountains. Or let both sides shoot it out until there is no-one left to fire a gun. Women should refuse to have sex and build a fort on top of a hill and take-up arms to defend their liberty. They should hang their veils as flags and let their hair catch in the wind.

Humour too, can be a feminist weapon to create a space for what is being denied as in Tiffany Tsao's 'The Sprig':

> I know how he'll unfurl.
> He will build empires.
> He will populate the earth.
> He will feed multitudes.
> He will shower the land with dollar bills.
> Then: a modest monument, a humble knighthood,
> a self-commissioned portrait hanging in the hallway.
>
> But let's keep this a secret
> or he'll never get over himself.

In Miriam Wei Wei Lo's poem 'Home' the diasporic dilemma is turned into a domestic one:

> Bed, toilet, kitchen. Exposed brick walls.
> This worn grey carpet, toys all over the floor
> reminding me that I have left the life of the mind
> for this. "Home!", the children call out in the car,
> "We're going home!" They must mean this place.

Chinese script is used in many of Wei Wei Lo's poems, not as an exotic gesture, but to emphasise the complexity of cultural signification. The acts of naming, writing and handwriting are translational, a portal of kinds, an opening up of the self, which can be exploited. This is referenced by Attamimi in 'Jaya's Exile' and by Eileen Chong in 'Lu Xun's Wife', kept illiterate and foot bound.

Merlinda Bobis crosses many thresholds of language. Her visceral trace from English to Pilipino to Bikol is metonymic of a return to the body before it has been traumatised by the coloniser. Body parts are often described as in the poem 'Covenant' which imagistically juxtaposes a bomb with a series of kite-flying amputations. Bobis peels back the potency of language as instrument of autonomy and subjectivity to appropriate, proselytise, seduce, convert. In 'Litany' the poet voices her grandmother's despair during an ISD call

> *hare ako pagbayae* —
> do not leave me
> as the wind leaves
> its tongue, thinned
> from howling
> do not leave me
>
> your wing, your eye, your ear, your tongue
> apprehend me—

That thirst for the mother tongue, for the taste of language is explored intuitively and with risk by female poets. Gita Mammen creolises language into a métissage of urban song and autobiographical surrealism. Alvarez and Li use grammatical inversions and omissions to make the texture of their verse disturbing and non-linear. Bobis often uses lower case as she weaves her way back to a pre-symbolic imaginary. This kind of language variance operates as a rhetoric of defiance and a reminder of the unstable nature of the hybrid spatial. Consider the mesmeric shifts in Li's sea voyage poems, the unanchored narrator in the ekphrastic 'Two children are threatened by a   , 1924'

Slippages between language, speaker, historical or domestic space disrupt the defining narratives of body and state, to reconfigure the concept of identity as one that is fluid, ambulatory and heterogeneous. 'We are *guest* people' writes Eileen Chong, 'without land or name, moving south and south,/wild birds seeking a place to call home.'

The very ambivalence of hybridity is harnessed to question *his*tory. In a similar way, Andy Quan's verse embodies a critique of straight culture and gender boundaries. His focus is the body, how it is sexed: the tongue in 'Queer and Odd', the legs in 'The Leg Crosser':

> *I also crossed my arms incorrectly*
> *like shivering instead of defence*
> *crossed myself profanely in church*
> *and my eyes, when crossed,*
> *frightened rather than amused.*
>
> *When I crossed my delicate fingers*
> *long and toothy and curved like crescent moons*
> *I wished for the unimaginable.*

Arguably, the more radical expressions of male/female boundaries are articulated by women, often in the first person. One poet, Dîpti Saravanamuttu, is regrettably absent from this anthology. Her poems dramatise the discursive aspect of multiple identities, situated in and transforming the body, often across geographical borders. To speak in the marginalised voice becomes by necessity a political act, even if compromised. Her radicalism deserves mention since it has inspired new voices.

Saravanamuttu appears in several Australian anthologies in which there are few other Asian Australian women. Many of these women have remained in the footnotes and peripheries of national canons, including those dedicated exclusively to women's poetry. Writing as foreigners in 'a male dominated subculture,' to quote John Tranter, (3) these poets have been twice excluded. Only two Asian Australian women appear in the *Penguin Book of Australian Women Poets* (1986); one appears in *Windchimes* (2006) in contrast to four Asian Australian men; and only three in *Motherlode* (2009). While ostensibly the feminist project has entered a postmodern mainstream, such gaps point to a more general invisibility in Australian poetry which we hope our anthology addresses.

From the uneasy discourses of multiculturalism in the 1980s and 1990s Asian Australian poetry has emerged as a strong, varied and highly accomplished field. The materiality of women's labour and the limitations of patriarchal spaces marginalise women within the body as a text; the text as a body, a space of counteraction from which to translate the present and to mediate the past. This crisis of belonging is a fertile ground that distinguishes them.

MICHELLE CAHILL

Notes

(1) Devleena Ghosh, 'Women in Asia', *Journal of Multidisciplinary International Studies*, Vol 3, No 2, 2006. http://epress.lib.uts.edu.au/ojs/index.php/portal.

(2) Ania Walwicz, cited in *The Penguin Book of Australian Women Poets* Ed Susan Hampton and Kate Llewellyn, Penguin Books, 1986, p. 1.

(3) John Tranter, review of *The Penguin Book of Australian Women Poets* Ed Susan Hampton and Kate Llewellyn, *National Times*, Sunday, 24 August 1986.

Alexandria

(for George Alexander)

At the mouth of the Nile
a Byzantine dome of many colours
defies its modernist renovations.
A sky the colour of a carnal life
kept moist with preservatives,
now too complete
fresh and a little sour like half dry acrylic,
authentic as the esplanade breeze,
the smell an index of cultural success:
rot, seaweed in withered bays.

That's why we come here to write:
the tired eyes of bachelors
track their favourite youths.
Fathers look for sons,
whom all the gold in Egypt won't beautify.
Gracious elderly waiters with colonial manners
affect a stance so long held,
wait as long as you do,
wait *with* you, your choice of refreshment
defines the gesture and makes the day.

Watching thunderstorms
assemble for battle out to sea,
from the balcony, a golden light
guilds the shabby roofs.
Is it dangerous to open all the doors
test the hinges on shutters? The way lightning travels
down telephone wires, through TVs.

Would my nose glow if hit,
would my head (suddenly blessed) wear a turban of plasma
in a cartoon version of Homer?

No appliances in this room, most basic
but... it's Egyptian enough, or is it
Greek – they never could make up
their mind, trapped between Kora standing to attention
and fantastic winged Gods.

Which is why, when I stare
at plaster cherubs in a sagging ceiling
I recall the museum of heavy-lidded
half bald consuls, the pallor of marble death,
the candy spiral of Venetian glass.

Or your childhood memory – Fremantle, 1956.
Airy epilogue, dusty essentials
at the end of the line
where the sea and the light
are now compressed
to layers of Pernod green,
and the epic goes to salt on the wind.

For Effendy, Emperor of Icecream

Effendy, I like the way you avoid work. It is saintly.
You stay up late, endlessly smoking on your porch
listening to the owls.
When we turn back on the freeway, we take a detour,
find strong tea in a maligned part of town.
Someone driving past in a Cadillac
reminds you of flat plains and cafeterias:
Ahh Utah! Big women of the prairies!

Back in the chai shop the light bulb factory workers gossip
and watch Tamil musicals on a giant Sony.
Lightning once struck the skewer
embedded in a Hindu's tongue.
Shall it do so once again?
But we are the virtuous and disconnected:
stroll about the kampong sucking toothpicks.
We made no ice-cream today you said,
with a look of triumph. Inshallah. Pray
for a sugar-led recovery; life so sweet
and sticky with discreet luxury.
We were never destined to make fighter jets.
Those yuppies need new flavours you said,
but I'm traditional. Tea is fine, or beer.
And home we went to 'Saving Private Ryan'
on your new DVD.

A Biography of 13

with a line by Wislawa Szimborska

And so the tour begins and ends
with luscious grammar school commentary:
"The North Sea wind blew across the Belgian mud
the flames rose in the German east."
Huddled in memory's dispatch box
Major Aitken buttoned up
his 13th Light Horse tunic.
No disgrace, he'd made it back,
from sniping Johnny Turk
to traffic duty at the Somme
to desk jockey on the Salisbury Plain
signing off on casualties,
supervising bayonet drills.

At ANZAC shrines in Melbourne
he'd pray with Presbyterian attention,
his BWM catching the sun,
and drink like the rest.

I swig a VB, the brand his father founded,
millionaire brewer
who left behind 13 children
and a will as long as this book.
I think of those to whom
the medals filter down.

13 years after V Day father went to Singapore
and bargained with a waif at Changi
for 13 postcards, "so cheap"
he just *had* to buy them.
His talents were letters, logistics,
advertising copy, wearing suits.
At the Office Party in Bangkok
he danced, quite pissed, in women's lace
then swapped the Major's "lucky" digger hat
for a pair of Dutch clogs.

When I was 13 my father left home.
Now I dream of a salt ghost
and recall the correct timing
when bells must ring, the melody for reveille
and other regimental habits
like whistles, or the cordite reek
of explosions, or what could make
the trench diorama more interactive
"when all the cameras have gone to other wars".

I think of how to honour a clerk
who became an auditor of destruction.

How he went to hell and back again,
like a number 13 horse (better than 8)
running on the luck they say it never brings.

Aubade 1

Wake up to hammering, a retching child
and Khmers getting married
with the official
Wedding Music Compilation
on a 72 hour loop and full volume PA.
To them silence is Hell.
A certain medication
will cure the child and
all your life will fit together.
One pill equals the average monthly salary.
Harmonious as a buzz-saw.
On the clef above
more sparrows and cockcrow,
bass drum and xylophones.
The maid drags the laundry into the sun,
the child is racked in spasm.
Or is it the neighbours
de-sexing the puppy
with a kitchen knife?
It's the underworld again, rumbling.
Temple thieves stand ready
to chisel out a dancer's face.
I reach out for the pills, shaking
with a fragile compassion. I mean
drink them down and nothing stays down
on mornings like this,
no doctor on my mobile.
Last night a hotel laser show blinded the hospital,

then it rained, thanks to Indra,
and it was possible, just possible
to keep on reading in the dark.

Aubade 2

Now I have been to China.
No more breaking 'the insteps
of wellborn Chinese girls'
to decorate escape memoirs.
Just a bang on the door at 6.
It's the party secretary's secretary
making sure I won't
miss the tour bus.

I would like to wake at daybreak
in a highrise on the sea.
In fact, there I would write more

at that hour, oh, of the dark suited men
smoking in the car park
and at the tomb of Confucius,
puffing on Double Happiness
among a thousand burial mounds.

Filial duty is a little boy
collecting coke cans for his Dad,
and for that he receives
a Double Happiness.

I would like to write more of the woman
who sold giant turnips of green skin
and purple flesh, which pucker your lips
with their pepper. I would like to write more

with their pepper and without
stealing your lines,
the ones that reek at morning's coolest
hour of day.

I wake in old "Funan".
It was clear to Zhou Da Guan (1296) why
the Khmers never travel at night.
They prefer to wake
at the earliest, and gather their nets, uproot
weeds at dawn, then resume
the chiselling of the frieze.
But they have no need
to write of waking, as far as I know.
There are no portraits of waking, none
of sleeping in the afternoon in empty
second hand bookstores.
But still they sleep as the world wakes.
It is a gift, to wake then, in old Funan,
to find oneself in thought.

The Wearer of Amulets

An old boy soldier you meet by the river.
And you ask him
why he never died.
He won't struggle for an answer.

There was a time
when all he'd thought of
was a winning lottery stub

and another time
a bullet whizzed past,

a voice had whispered duck
which he did
and the bullet
hit his friend.

And the Law of Karma said
his friend deserved it
while he himself had not.

A few days previous
in a post-lunch lull in the fighting
he'd knelt, chanting, on a wooden board
balanced on a bell
the shape of Mount Meru, sacred mountain,

while the friend espoused
a dull malevolence, forever searched
for a curse upon enemies;
remained unwashed,
avoided temple grounds,
would never pass the image of Buddha.

His friend would have killed the fortune-teller
who predicted the waning of his power.

Today, when I asked him
why he didn't die
the old boy soldier says
he aimed his AK at the Viets
and never missed
and boasts of killing conscripts
younger than himself;
how he'd tasted magic:
ivory, wild boar tusk

or a blended love philtre of oily liana,
dried python and the faeces
of a red vulture.

His friend who'd fallen
had worn a mother's milk-tooth amulet
a piece of gold of holy repute
round his neck —
a cheaper magic good for nothing

but for the good boy soldier
the best was a tattoo
of an inky mix of human bile
and the peeled skin of a monk,
or better still
a desiccated human foetus
cut from the uterus of a woman
pregnant three months;

the protector on a string
who would always whisper
advice and encouragement
through the din
of dangerous times;

a tiny, shrivelled thing
cleaving close to his heart, or held
between his teeth, as
the enemy charged in.

there's only ever been two

in our eyes' dilatory
dance our irises open
admit missed steps faults it marks
the corona every break
is here dot dot dash your bones'
brittle semaphore tattoo
out how far you fell how much
we have a third between us
a shift a shadow drawing
down the lids in noonday sun
shuttering hush of lashes
we say too much with fragile
instruments supreme geiger
counters tick tick tick burr
the needle swings don't you know
the meaning of it we dance
I lead you follow outside
are common house diamonds
winking out the clouds melting
a mushroom soaks in honey
the room whitens like a bone
exposed and we stand like posts
a thin string nailed between us
our eyes feel the heat shimmer
as something evaporates

En las montañas

echoes in the caves whistle clean through
some gypsy song splits the night in two
reaches the town
its multiple ears prick at the notes

houses above   necropolis below
skulls known by centipedes
bodies fleshy as a man's thumb

cave walls   softened
by the daily brush
of skin-covered bones

potsherds
dark ochre crumbling into dirt
who are the visitors here
transgressing between two spheres

rain rivulets fall down
like hair around a mouth
swallowing sounds

a finger moves from above to below
the low earth groans a song
dogs bark out to shadowed gods

The Pastoralist Speaks

At the edge of the close-cropped lawn
laps the drought, thirsty tongue all out.
Every change of name pocks its mark.
A scratch of smallpox on a survivor.
The squatters clear a small place.
A tongue licks dry lips.
A hand swats a fly, its buzz an airplane overhead.
All lawns a transplant, every ant a scavenger.
Under sod, a small tear, a drop of blood.
A bead of sweat collected in a dry swell
of pale earth. What birds wheel on Mulberry Hill?
On the face, carved eyes look down.
Make space. This land is too wide.
Plant feet on it to make it mine.

Curing the animal

My husband hands me the animal.
A soft neck roll and a dead eye,
a lustreless fur that I must touch
to strip and salt and peg to dry.
He is away all the day in the dust.
a eucalypt oil smell taints his neck
he comes to me
bones meeting mine
a hard fit
a green lawn at the edge of a desert
my heart, inexact
There is a sharp knife in the house.
I gather the wattle bark and boil it in a drum,
leave the skin to reek and call flies to it.
weeks pass, his eyes squint with distance,

monosyllables doled out, hard shillings
minted rare from his mouth, whiskers on his chin
scratch my skin. I pretend. Sleep.
Pulling one parsnip each, one leek.
The hard-fought cream, the butter's luxury.
The wallaby seasons its last useful night,
salt and pepper crusts its meat, the oil rolling
like mist off a morning.
Brown and sere of fat, it rests.
The marjoram rubs its scent on me.
The leek becomes soft, the parsnip tender
under butter. The meat drowns in gravy.
He chews 'til all the flesh is gone.
I pull the reddish hide from the reeking drum,
tip water to thirsty ground,
watch it drain.

In the Year of the Dragon

In the hour you are asleep, blackened embers
scar the moon and burn my old names. A lost girl

hungry for my tears dressed in china-blue knocks
on my door, a wild and naked boy

with cinnamon-brown skin grins and taps
on my windowpane. Flickering candles and wind-brushed

red leaves on fogged glass rouse me like a wounded
moth. I leave my crumpled bed. I stand wide-eyed in the chill

and see the shadows in the trees. At the height of March
the cold moon spooks me, the naked boy giggles

and plays his flute, the girl in china-blue
twirls and twirls holding a red book. The night air

cools my breasts and I hear
the ancient women and their old men whisper:

'There are no children here tonight, only ghosts
in boats rowing in their unborn lakes'.

The Last Drop   (*from* The Sisters sequence)

Khigala, my second child,
was born when the desert gods
sucked my milk
out of my plump breasts.
My love for her died when the last drop
of milk fell on my golden robe.

Although I wrapped her in my robe
the face of my child
became violet and prune-like. Without a drop
to drink, she screamed, but the hungry gods
just laughed. They jeer at breasts
that are empty of milk.

I prayed for milk
to seep through my robe,
fill up my breasts
and stop my child's
teeth turning mouldy blue. But the gods
refused me, and no drop,

not a single drop
of my mothering-milk
trickled out. The gods
sent me dreams of Lady Death in a red robe
mothering and stroking my child,
suckling her with breasts

leaking dragon blood. My breasts
began to ache, my nipples cracked, but not a drop
fell on her face. My child
never saw my tears, never tasted my milk
when I wrapped her tightly in my robe.
Oh, but the burning hands of the gods,

the hot winds beneath the gods,
how they have sealed the destiny of Seiyun! My breasts
and skin are now cold in this old robe.
White paint and black kohl that were dropped
years ago on my sleeves, remind me of spilt milk
and the icy cries of my child.

How do I forget the golden robe my child
once wore, and the day my breast-milk
dried as the gods sucked up the last drop?

Jaya's Exile

Once on the old port of *Sunda Kelapa*, Betawi
cradled the East Indies spices.
When tropical rain poured
over her plantations of mangosteen,
hibiscus, guava, nutmeg and cloves,
she would surrender
to the heat under her banyan tree
and sleep heavily.

In her youth, she bathed in the sap
of pomelo rind and her nipples were brown and salty.
The fleshy taste of mangoes on her breasts
and warm navel made her lovers return,
ravenous and bleary-eyed.

But over one dry season
her bones cracked, the day
a man arrived
wearing a suit, a black felt hat, navy tie
and a moustache
which he kept thinly lined.

He entered her, and changed her name,
he took her nights and bedded her each day.
He fed her wine and read her books
with long tedious words
till she ached for
her mother-tongue. She prayed

to *Sri Dewi* and made offerings
of ginger and mace. And when only moon tears
fell at dawn into her bowl, she watered
her fields and flowers with them for many months
until he sailed away, never to return.

She burnt his books,
and cocooned her son, tying his feet,
clamping down the echoes
of his father's words. On the eve
of Ramadhan, she stumbled on
her son, Jaya, hiding
by the banks of the Ciliwung. With her *kris*
she struck his ribs and banished him. Wrapped
in a sarong soaked in blood,
he left her shores
and roamed
unclaimed in every land.

Her earth looted and flooded, now
festered in cow dung and roaches.
The fence crumbled, nudged and eaten
by goats and mangled by weeds.
The Ramayana carvings guarding her gate
withered and chipped, attacked by rioters
in the ten-year war.

After many years in exile, Jaya
returned, an old man,
to his mother's island. Ashen faced,
yearning for her gaze, he found Betawi
slumped like an ailing beast at the foot
of a ruined minaret. Her breasts and stomach
rolled into one, veins of sweat
rivered neck and arms. Her head

had shrunk, her eyes sockets were holes
and her mouth had almost vanished.

Jaya knelt down
beside Betawi.
His words were muted, cuffed
by her raucous breathing.
When he pulled away from her breath
and wiped his reddened eyes,
he saw a day rooted in blood, his blood
gloving her fingers, his blood
mourning
the night he was exiled,
the day he spoke Dutch,
his father's uttering.

The 1740 Massacre of Chinese Immigrants in Batavia (old Jakarta)

The moon slowly rose over the riverside ghetto
on the eve of the festival for the Hungry Ghost. Crowds
on the banks of the Ciliwung welcomed
the dead with moon-cakes, they burnt gold money and lit
red lotus lanterns before releasing them down the river.

The old herbalist deafened her mind
to the festivities and shut her door.
She tucked a gulden coin in the cleavages of her *kebaya*:
the cost of treating the brittle-boned and dying,
and all night rolled one hundred

rice-paper scrolls. While she prayed for her dead,
those ancestors who had written the secrets in Indian ink,
her hands would glide over the cursive
Chinese scripts. A haze of burning incense
flowed through the room like a blue veil.

On the Day of the Hungry Ghost, she placed
scrolls with the recipes for love spells,
the remedies for rickets and tropical madness
in tight wooden boxes. The day Dutch soldiers
came and torched the riverside homes

the old woman reburied the heirlooms
under her carambola tree.
She heard her people scream, saw her shrubs burn.
Her tree, its roots and the red soil singed.
When the stilt legs of her river hut had cracked,

and walls were spitting out flames,
she flung her jades into the Ciliwung.
For a clean, prosperous death, the herbalist
placed a white bag over her head, pulled the string tightly
around her neck, and plunged into the river.

Waiting for Freedom

Down a blurred alley off Serangoon Road
in view of *Perumal* temple,
five headed bells ring
        waking the sleepless sleep
Familiarity within unfamiliar corners
        strangers begin to lose their shadows

Courtesy of a spaceless room—windowless
shoulder to shoulder, the six of us
Staring at the dim of ceiling
waiting for words,
        madam from the mansion

Through the racket
        rough love making from the neighbouring room,
father firms: *"freedom awaits in a new land,*
our futures"
        —away from the death knot of civil war,
common obituaries,
the unforgiving sharpness of a knife
She screamed finale—a long *aaahh!*
        a moment of freedom felt by all

Dressed with a thin noose
the interview at High Commission
Raised to answer every question
in little known language of English
Yes madam, even though it ought to be no at times,
she smiled at my village-school politeness

Father forced to turn home
five unguarded left on our own
        —the bells kept their heightened blare

Months passed, so did my case of puberty
Sympathetic strings of sitar,
our story in a melodious eulogy
Unable to meet the rent
sought asylum from the unknown
Perumal stood his solitary stance
unheard of our pleas

Living on *milo bungkus*
and daily dollar of curry puffs
Counting the number of passing cars,
drunken men who sing their misery on Indian streets,
wiping the tears of mother
(I had grown—
faster than the roaming clocks)

Month after month
under the lowering opaque ceiling
we waited—shoulder to shoulder
for a letter of freedom

Month after month
under the lowering opaque ceiling
we waited—shoulder to shoulder
for a letter of freedom

The Zoo

i
Fate of war—shunned
to a strange land
'Paradise' said the coloured brochures
Refuge for the abandoned,
            honeymoon pictures

Left at unversed doors,
new mother, a father—fern trees
Skeletal abode (a two-room home)
Six *'curry-munchers'* crammed (given
names)

ii
Solitary walk to school (a week late)
Shortened route through Saint Francis church
And in crucifixion
      Christ smiled at the new boy
Across the painted gravel (black followed
white)
Arrival with the street flash of amber
      next to ghosts of raised collars
Vultures in little clusters
Barely spoke theirs (English)
Blank across the muddy face
Stared by blondes and the blue-eyed—
      day at zoo
Fame spread to the knotted fence (all in a day)
I wilted
      kowhai at midday

iii
Dragged along the sports field
Dye of cut grass,
the habitual stain
Face below the bolus clouds,
      chewed away
Midrib's aches—courtesy of nameless stouts
The weathered knees—size eleven shoes
Spat on the frameless face; a freckled senior
Chased daily by the two-legged hound
Living on the same street

with a black dog—his absent father
Brochures of paradise
        pealing on the bedroom walls

iv
Mother battled (once a believer)
Father struggled (still does)
        a liberated prisoner imprisoned
Sisters fared (better)
        reversing eastwards over rising mound
Little brother (a chameleon who crossed the sea)
Instead I,
        lived / died / lived (barely)
Worse than war! (my morning anthem)
Harnessed a glare
        Soiled words
A borrowed face
Self—
        no longer mine
Even my shirt; gift of a kind woman

v
Days turned the pages of solitary memoirs
Hamilton's winter fell
over the departed mind
Firewood burned steady
Anger pruned the neighbourhood trees
And painted the empty walls
Fog mourned over the distant mile
Blowing mist; permanent numb
First two years
        couldn't afford the school jacket

My Country, My Lover

My country,
goddess of adulate flame
Craved by men and yesterday's youth,
her countless lovers
Slumber of scented hills
Bathed dress-less
in thrust of Indian Ocean
Architecture of her European conquerors
caught in curls of frangipani edges
Mahogany breasts in your palms,
secret passages of jackfruit honey
Her long neck
            curved guava leaves

Drunk on her southerly,
I weep
My country, my lover
misled by her lovers
An orphan child
sold and bought in abandoned alleys
Without defined tongue,
speaks in smothered hollow of hush
Her stitched lips
Forced by men of buried hands,
imagery impaired
Bruises—poisonous firm holds
Jaffna lagoon bleeds—weeps
from within to the nude shores
            never held

My country, my lover
like my first love,
            died

—in ledge of my chest
Crumpled rag and I,
    the creased servant
Thrown off the berm of eroding clutches
by robed sages growing devotion of odium
Her face in a veil
divorced from podium of speech
World chose instead,
comfort of venetian blinds
At wake, my shuteye
below the lowered knees
in cobras' glare
    my country, my lover
    my hands are chained

Smoke of Zebu

Grandfather turned the land
with a pair of humped bulls
Too young to lead the plough
I watched,
    spotted coat and short horns
Dung of bull; blood of his ancient breath
A boy I watched,
    fall of red stained sweat

Father turned the land
with a mechanical bull
Red tractor that ploughed the path
Too young to turn the wheel
I watched,
    treads of the beast; ascend of tipper's axel
Smoke of zebu; blood of his young breath
A boy an inch taller

DESH BALASUBRAMANIAM

I watched,
        rise of red filled sweat

Years in exile,
grandfather's ashes turned
to a palmyra palm
Father withdrawn
beneath beat of an aged heart
In an anonymous land
no longer a boy,
rather an unshaved man
Held to bones of his flesh
—I watch

men of immortal minds
masked in pureness of white
Turn the land
—a liberator's salute
Plough the loyal breeze
Erasing the fallen history
I watch,
ploughing through pages of a pen
As they turn my blood
filled with corpses
        who once had a name

This is where it begins

Once upon a time in Bikol, Pilipino, English— we tell it over and over again.

Digde ini nagpopoon. Anum na taon ako, siguro lima.
Si Lola nag-iistorya manongod sa parahabon nin kasag
Na nagtatago sa irarom kan kama.

Dito ito nagsisimula. Anim na taon ako, siguro lima.
Si Lola nagkukuwento tungkol sa magnanakaw ng alimango
na nagtatago sa ilalim ng kama.

This is where it begins. I am six years old, perhaps five.
Grandmother is storytelling about the crab-stealer
hiding under the bed. Each story-word crackles
under the ghost's teeth, infernal under my skin. I shiver.

But perhaps this is where it begins.
Grandfather teasing me with that lady in the hills
walking into his dream, each time a different
colour of dress, a different attitude under my skin.
I am bereft of constancy, literal
at six years old, perhaps five.

Or, this is where it begins.
Mother reviewing for her college Spanish exam:
"Ojos."
"Labios."
"Manos."
Suddenly also under my skin, long before I understood
"Eyes": how they conjure ghosts under the bed,
"Lips": how they make ghosts speak,
"Hands": how they cannot be silent.

I remember too Father gesturing, invoking
once upon a time. This is where it begins.
Story, word, gesture
all under my skin. At six years old, perhaps five.

And so this poem is for my father, mother,
grandmother, grandfather and all the storytellers,
the conjurers who came before us. They made us shiver
not just over crab-stealers hiding under the bed
or a lady uncertain of her garb. They made us shiver
also over faith, over tenderness.
Or that little tickle when a word hits a hidden
crevice in the ear. Just air
heralding the world or worlds that we think
we dream up alone.

No, storytelling is not lonely,
not as we claim—in our little rooms lit only
by a lamp or a late computer glow.
Between the hand and the pen, or the eye and the screen,
they have never left, they who "storytold" before us,
they who are under our skin.

Perhaps they even conjured us, but not alone.
Storytelling, all our eyes collect into singular seeing,
our lips test one note over and over again,
our hands follow each other's arc, each sweep of resolve.
Eyes, lips, hands conjoined: the umbilical cord restored.

Driving to Katoomba

Today, you span the far mountains
with an arm and say,
"This I offer you—
all this blue sweat
of eucalypt."

Then you teach me
how to startle kookaburras
in my throat
and point out Orion
among the glowworms.

I, too, can love you
in my dialect, you know,
punctuated with cicadas
and their eternal afternoons:

"Mahal kita, mahal kita."

I can even save you monsoons,
pomelo-scented bucketfuls
to wash your hair with.

And for want of pearls,
I can string you the whitest seeds
of green papayas

then hope that, wrist to wrist,
we might believe again
the single rhythm passing
between pulses,

even when pearls
become the glazed-white eyes
of a Bosnian child
caught in the cross-fire

or when monsoons cannot wash
the trigger-finger clean
in East Timor

and when Tibetans
wrap their dialect
around them like a robe

lest Orion grazes them
from a muzzle.

Yes, even when among the Sinhalese
the birds mistake the throat
for a tomb

as gunsmoke lifts
from the Tamil mountains,

my tongue will still unpetrify
to say,

"Mahal kita, mahal kita."

Covenant

after you bomb my town
I'll take you fishing
or kite-flying or both

no, it won't hurt anymore
as strand by strand, we pluck
the hair of all our women
to weave the needed string—
oh isn't this a lovely thing?

now hurl it upwards, mister

and fish that missing
arm-kite of my mother
leg-kite of my father
head-kite of my sister

perhaps, they'll ripple
the blue above your head
perhaps, they'll bite just right
to grace your board and bed

      arm-kite of my mother...

from wrist to halfway
above the elbow curved
as if still holding me,
the arm-kite

has no inkling
of its loneliness

when was it orphaned
from its hand that once
completed an embrace
and from the rest of it

before it flew
beyond retrieval?

leg-kite of my father...

it is my father
this knee, calf and half a foot
carved to new design

here, a muscle curlicued
there, a tendon filigreed
almost to perfection

but let me tell you, mister
the butcher at the market
does better art than this

head-kite of my sister...

not that she's rude
forgive her, sir
my sister just can't help herself

she has fallen
in love with staring
head-kites are hopeless like that

but they make up for it—see, where the neck
is severed, it is red and blue,
patriotic colours no less
like where you pin your medals on

arm-kite of my mother
leg-kite of my father
head-kite of my sister
rip-pling the blue

kite and fish or both
but always game

like the greener island to your south
that needs defending
or the white dove roosting
on that scrap of metal
with which you prop
your chin, so it could tilt
at the right angle of honour

how it gleams like hope
and rectitude

streamlined as only metal could be
in the hour of kites

Litany

hare ako pagbayae —
do not leave me
as an angel leaves
its wing, forgotten
in a bus about to pull
into a night with no moon

hare ako pagbayae —
do not leave me
as the moon leaves
its eye, lost
in a pool dreaming
of the dark without doors

hare ako pagbayae —

do not leave me
as the dark
leaves its ear, plucked
by the wind praying
to them who left too early

hare ako pagbayae —
do not leave me
as the wind leaves
its tongue, thinned
from howling
do not leave me

your wing, your eye, your ear, your tongue
apprehend me—
or was it i
who conjured you
in my belief

in flight, sight, hearing, song?
looming-hiding like a fickle cloud

[Author's note: 2003. On the phone in Australia to Grandmother in the Philippines, over and over I try to say goodbye. But each time, Grandmother, paralysed and unable to speak, suddenly finds her voice: "*Hare ako pagbayae, hare ako pagbayae*" — Do not leave me, do not leave me. She chants her distress. Over and over.]

Siesta

Take me not
in mid-winter,
only to thaw the frost
of your old bones,
imagining how stallions rear

in the outback,
hooves raised to this August light,

kakaibang liwanag,
kasimputla't kasinglamig
*ng hubad na peras.**

But take me
on a humid afternoon
made for siesta,
when my knees almost ache
from daydreaming of mangoes,
tree-ripe
and just right,

at higit sa lahat
mas matamis, makatas
*kaysa sa unang halik ng mansanas.**

---

*"alien light,
as pale and cold
as a naked pear"

plucked from my tongue you have wrapped
in a plastic bag with the $3 mango
from woolworths
while i conjured an orchard
from back home—mangoes gold and not for sale, and

*"above all,
sweeter, more succulent
than the first kiss of the apple."

Stamp Collecting

Starting with Australia, she slides the stamps
behind the filmy strip, the album breathing
promise in its fresh gluey feel, the world
being collected and unfolding as it fills up
shelf by shelf. As her five-year-old fingers
gingerly slip the countries into place, the questions
spill out, like the stamps from an old album
I opened yesterday, forgotten pressed flowers
of a time when the world arrived
in a philatelic queue, surviving
emblems from my stamp-mad phase.
Is Australia our home?
What is this country? Why doesn't it exist
anymore? Why is the Queen's face
on the stamps of so many nations?
We finger an atlas
of vanished countries: the CCCP, Yugoslavia
East Germany, Rhodesia, Malaya,
my childhood coming into place
under her learning fingers.
I remember the thrill as my fingers walked
the filmy rows, past the flora and fauna,
the faces of presidents and royalties,
gleaning a sense of a world out there
from the passage of stamps.
Those were my first travels,
transported on those serrated tokens
beyond the one-room flat
in Geylang Bahru
to the origins of those couriers.
The years of collecting culminated
in three bountiful, loaded albums,
tokens that brought those countries,

their histories and languages
to my fingertips.

I want to bequeath my daughter the albums
whole, the worlds I found and arranged,
but they have diminished to this half-filled, yellowed
album, proudly marked 1973, owned
bilingually in English and Chinese.
A few stamps have slipped from their moorings
and some lodge in the wrong countries;
others like the Burmese row still sit
faithfully in place. The missing ranks lost,
like many other things,
in transit, between houses, countries
and lives.

But in a strange way they are here,
all of the missing stamps and years,
the way those vanished republics
emerge in the atlas with new names,
present as my daughter picks
the last of a Singapore series
when it was still part of Malaya,
fingers the face of a youthful Elizabeth
pendant over a Chinese junk,
and slips it home.

Plum Blossom or Quong Tart at the QVB

Stroke by labored stroke my daughter
is discovering the sound of her name,
the new old country revealed under
her tiny preschool tentative hand.
She prints the pictogram *mu*,

a solid vertical stroke like a tree trunk,
a horizontal across for the arms, and a sinuous
downward branch on either side. That is
the radical for wood or tree. And on its right
she prints *mei*, meaning *every*, made up from a roof
over the pictogram for mother, *mu*,
with its nourishing embrace. Grafted on
the tree, it adds up to the talismanic
plum, tree and blossom.
It has been years since I have written
my true name. Watching
it appear in my daughter's wavery hand
I am rooted, the calligraphy
performing strange magic.
No longer emigrant, foreign
but recalled home, and not to the country
left behind, but further back
beyond the South Sea.
Vague lost connections
somewhere south of the Yangtze.
Karst country, paddies
and mountains the color of jade

My daughter asks why the English
transliteration is *Boey* and not
Mei. I am stumped.
Many Chinese names
became strange or lost
in the crossing.
How did the first *Mei*, arriving
with his mother tongue in the colony,
find himself rechristened
Boey? How long did it take
him to grow into the name?
Did he shed it like his queue?

Did he roll it in his mouth, taste
its foreign plosive, swallow it
whole like a ball of rice,
and spit it out *Boey*,
the pig-tailed coolie in the new colony?

In a few years my daughter will press
for her family history and tree
and I will have nothing more to show
than the withered branch that is
her dead grandfather. So much
buried, irretrievable. It is too late
to ask my father about his father and the father
before. Broken branches. So little history
to go on. One of the homonyms
for *mei* is nothing. *Mei* as predicate
to another character erases
that character. The same rising tone
spells bad luck
which runs in the family, it seems.

Perhaps the plum will flourish
on this soil, like the white plum
in our yard, and transplanted,
my daughter can recover
what is lost in translation.
Perhaps she already has.
Last week, at the Queen Victoria Building,
we stumbled on an exhibition
of the life of Quong Tart, the Chinese
pioneer who made it good in White
Australia. A tea merchant,
he married a Scotswoman, sang
Border ballads and wore tartan kilts;
he fed the Aborigines

and played cricket with the whites.
The catalogue printed his original
name *Mei*, our clan. His face,
a replica of my father's,
high cheekbones and well-shaped jaw,
had the same charming look. It was my father
made Mandarin of the Fifth Order,
costumed in silk tunic and plumed hat.

Somewhere in south-east China
the clan lived in the same village,
and broadcast rice seed
into paddies of broken skies.
Straw-hatted, they bowed
over plough and mattock,
planted in their reflections
like their name. Then news
came of richer harvests over
the South Sea, the white devils
and their burgeoning empire.
Perhaps great-grandfather sallied forth
with Quong Tart on the same junk,
and disembarked in Malaya, while Quong Tart
continued south. Perhaps they were brothers.

I see the other life my father could have had
staring out from the sepia shots,
if our forebear had travelled on
down-under. I could not explain
to my daughter the déjà vu, but her hand
was already pointing out the *Mei*
below Quong Tart's portrait,
the tap of the finger
wiring us, connecting us
in a tremble of recognition.

She has finally learned
the character of her name.

Clear Brightness

The house and yard dressed in a skin of ash.
It was raining embers, the night air thronged
with giddy petals that swirled
on the updraft, flared
to incandescence before curling into papery
ash, as we fled around midnight, my son
bewildered in my arms, his sister bright-eyed,
exclaiming, *It's snowing*, Christmas just weeks away.

We sweep the aftermath like penitents, the air
acrid, shriven, ashen, as it was on the day
of Qing Ming, Clear Brightness, in another life,
when families filed to the tombs with broom,
rice wine, boiled whole chicken and fruits, and stacks
of paper money, gold and silver currency
valid only in afterlife. The dead were fed,
their abodes swept, and the filial queue
of joss offered. Then the money was given
in fanned reams to the flames, transferred
to replenish the ancestors' underworld credit.
Once Grandma brought us to the cemetery,
dragging us in tow with armfuls of offerings,
filing up and down the crowded ranks
for the right address. I don't remember whose grave
it was we were tending, or Grandma telling us
to pray. Only a blurred oval photo of a man
on the worn headstone, and the hundreds of fires
around us, the air swimming
with ash-drifts, the sun eclipsed in the smoke

but its heat made more palpable by the pall
that hung over the day. I imagined the ancestors
catching the burned money like willow catkins, turning
them into real millions that they could send back
to us to bail my father out of bankruptcy.

Now grave news from the living I have left;
the cemeteries are dug up, razed, the dead
expelled, their bones unhoused, ashed
and relocated to columbaria to make
room for progress. No more tomb-sweeping
and picnicking with the dead.
No such unrest for Grandma and Dad
who went straight into the fire.
Anyway they turned Catholic
and have no use for paper money
or earthly feasts.

Here the bush is charred, the trees
splintered, pulverised like Dad's bones
after the fire. The ash taste clings
to the house, even after hosing and sweeping.
It seeps into my dreams, into the new life
I have made, and on my sleep it is still raining
ash, flakes falling like memory, on my dead settling
like a snowdrift of forgetting

La Mian in Melbourne

On Little Bourke Street it's the bewitching hour
of winter dusk's last riffs playing
long mauve shadows down the blocks,
waking the neon calligraphy, its quavering script
mirrored on the warm sheen of the Noodle King

where a man slaps and pummels the dough
into a pliant wad. He takes a fist-sized ball
and starts his noodle magic, stretching the bands,
the sleight-of-hand plain for you to see,
weaving a stave of floury silent music.

You stand islanded from the passage
of bodies and cars, the art of *la mian*
reeling you in to a music deep beneath
the murmur of traffic, beyond the fusillade
of a siren down the street. Between here

and wherever home is the noodles stretch,
sinuous, continuous, edible songlines multiplying
into a cat's cradle of memories, the loom-work
of hands calling to the half-forgotten hum,
hunger for what is gone, the lost noodle-makers

of the country left behind:
the *wanton mee* hawker in Tiong Bahru,
the *mee rebus* man on Stamford Road,
and Grandmother serving long life
noodles for each birthday, her deft hands

pulling three generations under one roof.
The noodles were slightly sweetened to ensure
the long years came happy, not like Grandmother's
difficult eight decades, the family dispersed
at the end, the ritual of birthday noodles lost.

Now you watch the handful of hand-pulled
noodles dunked in a boiling pot, then scooped
with a mesh ladle onto a waiting bowl of broth.
You sit before it, enveloped in steam,
chopsticks ready to seize the ends
or beginnings, and start pulling them in.

Kālī from Abroad

Kālī, you are the poster-goddess, sticking out your black
tongue, like Gene Simmons from Kiss, a kick in the teeth,
with your punk-blue leggings, your skull-and-scissor charms.

You swing a trident, a demon's head, and dance on the bones
of a pale Śiva. I recall the convincing eyes of a girl cripple
carrying your bottled effigy, as our bus careened to a dusty halt.

Some say you morphed from Pārvatī, drunk on blood,
others cite your superhero leap from Durgā's brow to slay
the self-cloning serpent before a Haka dance on mythic soil.

By a hundred Sanskrit names, India claims you in a single text,
while in *Zen and the Art of Motorcycle Maintenance*, you are
'the grass and the dew', on screen, our contemporary Judge Judy

having a bad hair day. I'd argue for your cosmopolitanism,
a global denizen, you're adroit in drugs and aphrodisiacs, a nude
dominatrix, a feminist export with a sadomasochistic bent.

A figure of partition you were cover girl for *Time* magazine.
A neo-pagan diva, your wholeness is darkness fashioned
from light, moon-breasted, with eyes of fire, with Brahmā's feet,

Varuna's watery thighs. You rise from the grave, step over
carnage, feeding the world and your severed self with blood.
Stripped bare as Duchamp's Bride, you set bachelors in motion.

Pārvatī in Darlinghurst

So I lay on the body of a pale Śiva. He spoke
not a word, bothered perhaps by my nut-brown
skin, my slow dance calmed his electro shuffle.
A slap of limbs pinned him down to my earth.
I hadn't bathed in sandalwood, flouting legend
with a preference for Estée Lauder. The moon's
crescent tangled my hair, my breasts were bare,
our timing synchronised. Night fizzed, vanishing
into day, the club's hypnotic rhythms subdued.
We scorned the *Purānas*, our tryst no Himalayan
cave, but a hotel bed I had draped with stockings,
lingerie, and the crystal ice of a Third Eye. I admit
that's why I spoke with the speed of an antelope.
It seems the *acharyas* were mistaken: I hadn't
dated for marriage or adultery, nor with a wish
to deck his house with flowers or sweep his floors.
I am too busy, I declared, for dalliance or abstract
gossip. I have no interest in honeybees and birds.
All I wanted was a good time. I swear as the river
is my sister, that this guy was not my sun or my sky.
No way did it even enter my mind to have his kids.
His first wife's ashes are scattered all over the city.
Goddamn it, Śiva is a walking disaster; whatever
he touches burns. Restraining him with handcuffs
I said, 'Listen babe, your *lingam* and my *yoni* are
made for one thing only, improper and unchaste.
It's little more than conjecture to think our sweaty
helix could ever be whole.' Then I offered to grind
and gyrate him silly, suspend our want indefinitely,
and he fell utterly silent with this new meaning.

Ode to Mumbai

for Dilip Chitre, after his 'Ode to Bombay'

Piece by piece I'll remove your unwieldy syntax.
I'll taste your jaggery, as the street's kaleidoscope
triggers a new explosion. I'll tear up draft after draft,

while you scorn my attempts to write an elegy
or an epic. Not your first beggar or *bailadeira*, I, too,
am engendered, colliding with *hijras* who float like dark

moths weaving through Santa Cruz traffic. I'll find
relief in each disappearance and hallucination, discover
your tableau of devas, slumdogs, spivs and impresarios

is a divine smokescreen or a hologram that easily bends
into a new simile. But when held up to the light
I'm left with only negatives. Mumbai, even your name

is a philologer's conundrum, as mine is the antithesis
of my self, a colonial slip. Strip the layers, what remains
are the bones, a different grammar for equivalent parts

of speech, the same ivory teeth in any caste or creed. I
hang in a gap between the sound and meaning of words,
dipping my subconscious in different time zones, where

my bed is a temple and a brothel, where dream defines me.
Your poem has a history, in which my pages are missing.
I rise from the poem on a burning ladder of language.

Swans

Here in Orkney, they time-share as winter voyagers
undisciplined pacifists, neither sentinel nor apsara.
A splash of colour on the bill is tarred as a birch leaf,
refusing to fall. The eye keeps faithful to her sky gods
knowing the powder of white water, the Nordic crags.
The throat's dying tone is a clarion, to which I woke
one Arctic night, from my tent on the island. Against
the sky's green streamers they passed like gold leaf,
each captive pair, master and slave, returning to nest,
to feed on potato chats, the grain stubble. I knew then
no prayer or piety would convert these birds from patent,
territorial white. They are certain to hunger, to haunt
the estuaries in genetic script. There are no stichomythic
verses, no Viking battles or baptism in their dreams.

Day of a Seal, 1820

A tall ship patrols the coast,
                          pelagic fish are vanishing.
I sniff the kelp and bloodworms,
                          mould into an eroded kerb
with an awkward wriggle of neck, whisking
                          as if hiding my fur was natural
                          as instinct for milk or man.

Tuesday afternoon, Bass Strait's shadows
                          ring the slaughter sands.
A man in sandals reeks as he wheels his rage
                          with a pivot, swings his heft.
A half-caste. I watch him clench the haft,
                          before the first blow shocks.
                          He braces and repeats.

Black women from the camps pile our skins
                    on spits for tobacco, for oil.
Some grab at birds with their gloves— Now
                    I am weightless as feathers
my arteries shut tight, as if underwater,
                    the acidosis bearable though
                    I cannot strike back.

Love's Legend, a Sermon

"Let true affection shun the public eye"
— Mary Tighe

{ setting: a small square
near West Lake, Hangzhou
voice: singular

how across the square the
other one glanced also : | |
ever since remaining
crossed, each one
remains faithful (or
tries) to that crossed
glance which cannot
be forgotten, bisecting
the square with its
universal optics.

an enormous wave
of doves do the same,
all red-black, unleashed as if
they were the *cause* (after-
ing) of this inaugural
glance

if it is forever true,
I, numbered the third, am
not its cause: watching
from a distance, summoned,
neither one did I know.

nobody decides,
yet the glance

keeps going
eternally.

envoi

| |: neither have
    ever
       known

reading Mao in the future

while watching his body
,blowing my squeaky flute
then out in the snow
with my happy little sister
both of us with our flutes | |
save us from that holophrase lake! ♪
let's run away from
mummy and Mao
that greedy one behind
the glass who looks like
Two people at once, let's not
tell mummy we're having
dumplings if daddy said so
let's jump into this mighty
icy lake, get lost in it,
blow our squeaky
flutes, let's see the bones '
in Macau, don't tell mummy
,daddy let us in in in for
the Portuguese tarts
custard hot and milky for
the tummy — who knows,
may we drown in the long

lake underneath the pagoda?'
would mummy save us?
daddy would, let's not
ponder how later we
both played dead and...
I'm divided, inabhorably,
white bones remind me of father
and telling us mummy don't
blow the firecrackers
in my face, little sissy let's
climb behind the marble
statues and pretend mummy
can't see, daddy will protect
us from Mao reading [*selah*]
in the future or if we fall in
the icy lake and nobody
saves us!

Hong Kong, 1999

didn't feel the Century turning
at the heels of finitude's score
didn't feel the strings
Capital's orchestra
rumbling,   the

(whistle tune)

City watched me,
heard later the stammer
of hammers, Father spoke for

planes lurching round
the tablecloth mountain

did I
become a militant
when I glimpsed my cousin's
sex manual

stuffed between

the beds?

Learning to Leave

The streetlamps pass us like the years:
my father is driving me away

from our house on that street where
I learned about the shyness of the mimosa

plant, whose eyelids close
even in the faintest breeze.

This was where I learned to wait
for the bus to arrive to grow up

and patiently counted to a hundred
before going in search of the hidden.

This was when we crossed oceans
under tables to invented countries

but sought permission to go to the park.
I have packed my future in these boxes

that sit in the boot of the car now,
as we drive past the market that has since

been torn down. In its place is a lonely patch
of grass. On this night the roads seem wider

and emptier though I see a thousand tiny lights
ahead. In the car the anger of the traffic

cannot reach us. As the light turns green,
I wonder what my father catches in his rearview

mirror as I focus on the road we're moving along
wishing we'd never get there or return where

we were, wishing we could go on traveling

as the streetlamps pass and mimosas
open and shut their tiny palms

conquering their fears, as a song plays
on the radio, which will soon pass on to another song.

Miles

No, I don't know how many yards make a mile,
how many gallons we'll need for however far it is
to St Andrews, to Perth, and back; how many litres
a gallon, and how many pounds for that.
You're trying to understand the math behind this
getting there, having bought a map, hand on the wheel

as I think only about how it has been two months,
eight weeks, a million days or barely one since
we've met. *Did you read that sign?*
You ask, trying to place these fields,
this road, trying to remain in control.
I'm sure we're still on the A915, I reply,

the way I'm sure you haven't lost your glasses;
things don't just disappear. They're just waiting
to be found, somewhere else if not here, where
you haven't thought to look. Most things
aren't obvious or as clear. *How do you know?*
You ask. *How can you be so sure?*

The sea is somewhere near, I say.
From wherever we are off the map,
I can hear it breathing and sighing,
flinging itself against cliffs and walls,
or clinging on to some shore, before slinking
away reluctantly, in search of a somewhere else
that may give something more.

Away

The year I was born, we were meant to move
to Australia. As I cried in hunger for more milk
my parents waited for an answer.
For years my father searched
to leave. Every year we took trips,
someplace else, somewhere away.
I longed for home and my toys. Father wished
otherwise: that he would never have to go back
to the misunderstanding that is his life
in Singapore. There, the roads
taken were circular; always returning you
to where you were, always lost.

The year I left our country for Melbourne,
my father said, don't go. After that he found
himself in Istanbul; city of the world's
desire, city on seven hills,
one for each abandoned dream.
My father's heart was sold to the city
that belonged to two continents at once,
while I mailed mine back
and forth, between Singapore, my father,
and the places I've never traveled.

Popcorn

5pm, and I'm craving popcorn, one of those afternoons
that smell of warm rain that hasn't yet fallen, the smell

of warm, baked roads and the anticipation of a real good
wash-your-migraine-out storm. I want popcorn.

Popcorn in a bag from the margins of Bangkok, caramel crisp
coffee popcorn from that loved-up train station where

the corn-popper is also a barista who lovingly burns my coffee.
I'm sure she never drinks that filth. But she's not here

so I make do with cheap popcorn from 7-11. I almost miss her.
The bag says it's made in Singapore, product of America.

So much of what we eat and do is a product of America
and China. Just last week a Chinese migrant told me he's never

drunk canned Chinese herbal tea with his meal before. You're joking,
I said, surely you drink tea with meals. This isn't tea,

it's a soft drink, *qi shui*, he insists, and by the way
in China only white collared workers drink coffee.

His small eyes widen as he adds, *and the food here is inedible.*
Your people mix different foods together on a plate. It's all a mess

and tastes nothing like home. He should know; he's a chef back home.
I don't tell him that this is home on a plate for me, that in Melbourne

where I lived for four years, I missed this shit everyday.
He spends his days here slicing gourmet cakes, twelve hours a day,

in a factory I have never seen. Those delicate cakes sold in cafes
slicing up his hours, graying those small, surprised eyes.

But now this popcorn will have to do. It's too soft and plasticky,
tasting of nothing but 7-11 florescent lights

and first-world boredom,
human dreams.

Common State

What is it I'm fishing for
if not difference. What is there
but the hope this lack of fire,
these safe words will lead us
to what we cannot yet expect,
but expect to find.
Are we on the same side of the question,
or are you tracing a common state
meant for no-one but the future you think is possible,
the one I do not see. The moon tonight is an earring.
Why am I here wondering why I am here
with you in this dead silent country,
fishing, when what I want is to drink all this
air, and what I need is what is left after the fire,
not safe words or careful dreams of light.

On Seeing a "Uniquely Singapore" Advertisement in Australian *Vogue*

Expect only the new...

I'd like to meet she who wrote this.
Surely she knew, this too

gets old. I want to know where
she came from, where she has been, what she has read

and the lines she has written; who else reads her,
and through her words, imagine Singapores

new and old. I want to know if they can see
what it is without looking forwards or back,

or sideways at other lands.
This is not about mistakes or blame,

blood on hands. All I have are questions,
which roads to home, why the flood on tracks.

Chinese Silence No. 101

after Timothy Yu, "Chinese Silence No. 4"
after Billy Collins, "China"

I am a flattened spider inside a discarded book of Chinese poems
on the drawing board of a curious architect.

Grand designs are being drafted.
Many bottles of champagne await opening day.

But even when he's mad
and hurls the book across the room,

I stay as silently still as the dead,
unread words on these pages.

Chinese Silence No. 102

after Timothy Yu, "Chinese Silence No. 7"
after Billy Collins, "Liu Yung"

This poet of the Australian Chinese community is so agreeable.
Crowds sigh at his poetry readings,
birds overhead stop to listen
and asylum seekers steer their boats toward Australia.

If only he appreciated the living
he makes (compared with what I do) —
no dead-end full-time job,
no busking for gold coins

playing Neil Young's "Birds", no fear,
not even of the final press of the mute button.

Chinese Silence No. 103

after Timothy Yu, "Chinese Silence No. 8"
after Billy Collins, "Hangover"

If I were crowned Paramount Leader of China this afternoon
every peasant planting rice in a paddy field
would be re-educated and silenced forever
from uttering the name of Mao Zedong

Mao Zedong Mao Zedong

then would not be required to read *The Little Red Book*
but my *My Book of Thoughts*
and learn to spell Chairman Mao's name in English
in my preferred transliteration of

Mao Tse-tung Mao Tse-tung

after which they would be quizzed
about the spelling of his name then executed by firing squad
regardless of how little they retained
of their thoughts of how

Mao Zedong thought Mao Zedong Thought would be thought of.

Chinese Silence No. 104

after Timothy Yu, "Chinese Silence No. 11"
after Billy Collins, "Drawing"

Sampan on rusty river –
a curved wooden bridge
under a grievous sky

silence in the distance
and in the foreground
a hearing aid in each ear.

I turn to the east
to face the easterly
wind-blown silence rushing towards me.

Chinese Silence No. 105

after Timothy Yu, "Chinese Silence No. 6"
after Billy Collins, "Despair"

So little poetry in our gloomy silence,
our words are flattened temples,
earthquake-cracked mirrors of ourselves.

Our fully-clothed bodies cover the bed,
our moans lost eons ago through the chimney
to greet the silence of the heirs.

I wonder what my ancestors would make of all this
inactivity, this axe

to the family tree?

Tonight, with the libidinous moon mocking me,
my thoughts turn to the lost
children of the next generation:

Yu No Bee, who I would have wanted, in the great Chinese tradition,
to be either a doctor or a doctor, and who would have been
a great brother, I'm sure, to his younger sister,
Mi Sing.

My Hakka Grandmother

If time could unwind for you
yet be still for me, we would run
through the fields, feet unbound
and pummelling the ground towards

the earth-house. I read about it once:
its architecture unique to the Hakka people
in Fujian. Dwellings like wedding rings
stacked and interlinked. You would lead me

through the building's single gate
and show me where you slept, above
the communal granary. It would smell
of rice husks, like your dark hair

in the mornings before we'd braid it
long and sleek. I would speak
in your tongue, but we would not need
words. The lines on my palms mirror

yours almost perfectly. I wonder where
our bloodline begins. We are guest people
without land or name, moving south and south,
wild birds seeking a place to call home.

Lu Xun, your hands

"But as you look up and inhale the intoxicating smoke from
your tobacco, can you spare a thought for those scrambling
to find a way out of this nest of scorpions?"
— Xu Guangping, in her first letter to Lu Xun, 1925

Lu Xun, your hands
are clasped behind your back,
across the black silk
of your scholar's dress. My eyes trace the length
of your fingers encircling your wrist. Tonight,
Lu Xun, your hands will drag
their heavy, eloquent path across
my milk-soft skin. Your mouth will cease
to form words like *liberty, ideology,*
and *compassion* but will instead silently
enclose the peach blossoms
of my breasts.

Lu Xun, your hands are the instruments
through which you conduct
your desires. In the morning, your fingers are pale
and controlled; your brush hovers
then descends upon the undulating sheets
of rice paper. My eyes follow only
each stroke. Your thoughts
unfold before me, beginning
at the moss-green rocks. They linger
in the shade of the toothpick pavilion, beneath
its heavy jade tiles. They form a blood-red,
half-moon bridge

across the rush of river
fed by the waterfall whose origin lies
in the death-grey mountains. Lu Xun,
your hands warm the wood of the pipe
that I fill. My fingers, deft as birds
in flight, strike a match-soldier. Provoked,
it flares orange and ash. Dragon,
you exhale whole curlicues of cloud. Words
as yet unformed in my mind
now go up in smoke. They too know
that I am in heaven, Lu Xun,
for your hands.

Mid-Autumn Mooncakes

It's nearly mid-autumn. I spy the tins
at the Asian grocer — gaudy red peonies
unchanged for forty years. Of course
I buy the mooncakes with double yolks:

here in Australia, yolk or no yolk,
they cost the same. I should wait for you,
wait for the full moon, light some lanterns
and try to make out the lunar rabbit,

the Chinese fairy, but I don't. I cut
the mooncake into quarters and spoon
out the deep orange yolks, leaving
half-round cavities in the sweet

lotus paste. Eaten on their own,
the yolks are creamy, almost too salty.
A continent away, I imagine my mother
in her kitchen, slicing through shell

and briny white, remember my father scraping
duck eggs into rice porridge. They always saved me
the yolks. My bowl, a cradle of bright congee
full of the gold of the mid-autumn moon.

Winter Meeting

for Boey Kim Cheng

In the tepid winter sun we walk briskly
to catch a bus to Chinatown, my footfall
ten years behind yours. I'd closed
my eyes – a defence against a wellspring

of wet – when you spoke of *la mian*
in Melbourne that made you homesick.
We head for the promise of *mee goreng*
at Mamak's – conjuring late nights

of oil-sheened woks at Newton,
of flames in rings the size of giant plates
that lick at this Malay-named marriage
of Chinese noodle and Indian spice. Before

we arrive, the Sydney skies release rain
like the monsoon. We stand on a corner
under tin awnings, peppered by spray, watching
this familiar rain. The drains have had their fill

and creeks run like poetry escaping the page.
Unlike children, we skip puddles and try not to splash.
We are still strangers: under my small umbrella
you are half-drenched. An old song surfaces: *Wa neng nang...*

Inside, surrounded by smells of home, my tongue loosens
then slips into the cadences of Singlish. I tell you of the afternoons
my grandmother fried *sambal belachan* in the house. You wrinkle
your nose: these memories need neither grammar

nor elaboration. You offer me an antidote for sadness:
recite Wang Wei, Du Fu, Meng Haoran. But where you go
I cannot follow — I lost the language years ago. Outside,
the rain has stopped. We drink our tea and split the bill.

Grandmother's Dish

Buy the freshest prawns, grey ones
are the sweetest. Peel them, tails and all,
and save the shells, especially the heads.

Use your biggest pot. Heat some oil, then fry
garlic, whole cloves, and spring onion tied
into a knot. Add the shells and fry until they

turn pink. Now the pork bones. Add water.
How much? Enough. You'll know. Bring to a boil
then let it simmer until the water turns red.

Pluck the *tau gay* tails, all of them. We can do it
together while we watch the Taiwanese drama.
Cook the pork belly strips in the stock

until they are just firm enough to slice. Cut
the fishcake thinly, on a angle. Better that way.
Now the noodles: mix yellow and white. Fry

in the wok with garlic, add prawn, pork, fishcake,
fry some more, then add a little stock. Cover
and let it cook. Be patient. Good things must wait.

Add the *tau gay*, then crack the eggs into the dish
and stir. Add pepper and salt now, but only white
pepper from Indonesia. Angmoh pepper not nice.

Ask who wants to eat. Don't forget the sambal.
How to make sambal? That's another dish. Today
is Hokkien Prawn Mee. Eat now, while it's hot.

Lu Xun's Wife

I was his wife. It was not my fault
I was kept illiterate, that my feet were broken
into lotus buds. I was born to be a wife,
not a servant, and I was handpicked

for him and married by proxy. Like
a good woman, I lived as a daughter
to his mother. We shared rice and embroidery,
waiting only for the return of the man

who bound us both. I remember my first glimpse
of my husband. His hair was cropped
like the Japanese, but he wore the long gown
of a Chinese scholar. I wondered:

should I drape his robe across
the back of a chair, or leave it
in a gleaming puddle on the floor?
That night I waited in my bed,

shivering in red silk underwear.
The wedding candles burnt down
and the date tea grew cold,
but he did not come for me. Night

after night he spent with his books,
and still I waited: bathing, dressing,
undressing. I have been kept ignorant,
but I know this: his hands have never

caressed me the way he lifted brushes,
spread ink, stained paper. I can write
my name: *Zhu An*, and our surname,
Zhou. I do not know who Lu Xun is.

CHRISTOPHER CYRILL

Extracts from *Quaternion – a prose poem novella*

1. In Dore's *Illustrations for Dante's Inferno*, the minotaur *on the border of the broken chasm* (Plate 32) is himself broken. Neither Virgil nor Dante grieve or rejoice at his bereft posture – he is no longer a threat to poets or virgins or heroes – they are dispassionate observers. I cannot forgive their objectivity. The observers could have put a hand out to the wracked beast, or at least assisted it towards a dignified death. Or so I imagined at the time. I have not seen the woodcuts for a decade.

2. I had three uncles once, my mother's brothers. Charles called Chuck, Elvis and Theo. The pose of the minotaur I remember from Dore's engraving is the same pose I see when I imagine my uncle Theo's body lying on a traffic island the night before his wedding to Teresa. The observers – his pursuing, elder brothers – one soon to be searching the streets of Little Luck for a pay phone, the other with handcuffs, shaving cream, a silk garter in his hands – look upon the ruined body with expressions of terrible contrition. (There was a third witness whose identity I could never verify.)

3. No doubt my grandfather would have threatened the *boys* – they were all in their twenties then – with a beating, then disinheritance, then with the wrath of Job's God. He would have said they deserved divine anger more than any form of forgiveness their mother would flatter them with. He would have blighted their names for the hours they had consigned her arthritic knees to the pew before the eyes of Jesus Christ.

4. My grandfather would have called the Parish priest before the ambulance. He would have settled, as surely as we all did that night, upon death as the inevitable outcome. For him, I imagine, it would have been more important to save the souls of the still living sons before he prayed for the dead one to be recommended unto heaven. Then he would have called one of my aunts to fill my grandmother's syringe with insulin.

5. It had ended in the needless – *careless* – way the sisters had predicted that afternoon, soaking lentils, skinning ginger and crushing tomatoes for the next day's feast. It had ended with the exact, predicted outcome that the carousing and drinking and *carrying on of the boys, careless boys*, would lead to. *Dressing up the hall now so they can drink rum longer, let's see whose eyes open before noon.* Death, settled upon by all of us, before the ambulance arrived to Little Luck. (Even when the uncles were grown, church-going fathers and full time workers, they would be criticised for their irresponsibility. Horses, dogs, cards, brown rum, white rum, Vat 69, girlfriends *on the sly* and then another girl for weekends.)

6. Theo was not dead. His leg was broken. He was not the first son my grandfather would bury but he would bury the two elder sons, complaining his own coffin would be made of cardboard. My grandfather would have identified the need to have the remaining boys chastised before they resorted to any kind of further foolishness, some theatrical act of contrition not even the sisters could imagine. (Chuck had once beaten his arms with a stick as punishment for taking the Lord's name in vain.)

7. By the time the other drunk men had arrived, brought out unsuspecting to view the accident of some stranger – they would have chased had they not been too drunk – or by the calls of the weeping pursuers, the news would have been brought to the rest of us. The celebrations were only two streets away – inside Little Luck. All our neighbours would have known within the hour. All would be asked to pray to St Jude the following Sunday. That is how I imagine it, I cannot say truly what happened and no one has ever told me. I was eight years old and barred from the bachelor party.

8. However, it is true that I witnessed my mother say, when the car screeched and before the screaming started – the sound of the impact did not reach us – *Theo.* For a moment, between the screech and the screaming she must have felt relieved. We lived in Little Luck but one

street from the home of my grandparents, a further street away from the roundabout where the four Ink streets – north, south, east and west – met.

12. I cannot explain the origins of our family superstition that weddings foretold bad luck and funerals good. We believed the betrothed were harpies of misfortune, the dead deliverers of prosperity – in health, honour, income tax returns. I presume it came from some chance occurrence generations back and what had begun as a story of wild circumstance had evolved over the years into a prophecy – a heart attack as a ribboned car entered the street, three straight hands of blackjack in the game at a wake, the kitty halved and shared with the widow. Even though I disbelieved the superstition I could never quite disavow myself of it, in the same way I could never cut paper at night – this rained black words upon our house – or leave a wallet completely empty – this whistled destitution to our front door.

14. I reasoned that the superstition of weddings and funerals had overtaken common sense, that make believe had by then overridden all the evidence that disproved it. It was not our only superstition but as there was a wedding or funeral procession almost every week in Little Luck it was the one that caused the men to put an extra five on race eight or the women to cross themselves and pray a rosary at the sight of a hail of confetti or a rented horse and carriage, despite also feeling obliged to pay respects or register a gift. At the time of the accident I reasoned that Theo's wedding could not have caused the misfortune. It had yet to occur. If Theo had died, no wedding would have taken place and hence no possibility of mischance. But to question this superstition seemed a form of blasphemy.

17. One of the partygoers delivered the news, doorway to doorway. My mother and I walked down Lucida St, toward the scene. Every second streetlight flickered, as if tapping out signals in some coded language to a faraway observer. The wind turned the drizzle in circles around the lights. We held hands. She was humming beneath her breath. Her cheeks were striped by rain. She seemed to me then like a river landscape. I began to

imagine she was leaving me too. She had told me my father would be home less and less — because of the job. *He has many things on his mind now and you must not ask why, why?* And this, I thought, was our goodbye walk. At the next turn she would go left and I would go right and as we moved away from each other we would remember all that had happened between us and consign those memories to a past that would seem in years to come to have never happened. The language of light above us coded this to a faraway observer. Whoever was watching could see what I imagined.

18. We walked to the roundabout that linked the four Ink streets. A few men were still standing there as if marooned. Glass twinkled in the gutter, the ambulance had come and gone and there was some blood on the grass.

20B. My wife, Alba, one night, as a car passes through the street and U-turns and the headlights pass through the bedroom and we both wake and wonder whether the light has woken the child, says:

You hold their tiny hands in yours finally after all the kicks, the nausea, the blood tests, the gel before the amnio, the small ghost floating on the screen, that same fleshed out ghost inside you. And then you learn the Heimlich manoeuvre, learn to recognise the first signs of measles, learn to identify the toys they could swallow, the avoidance of grapes, the statistics of drowning, the chances of whooping cough. You take the blue book everywhere. You have them immunised but a limp, a lump, a weeping sore keeps you awake at night and you disregard the burning of your own sleepless bones to administer drugs, to hold them down by all fours to get the painkiller into them. Just to sleep to wake and change the greenish nappy at three am and give the next hellish dose. Less TV, more vegetables, check the sugar content in jam, and all the time you are sure you are doing a poor job, your heart cracks every time you lose your patience. No ring on your finger, people notice that. But really it is just you preparing for their imminent death, you are always imagining their deaths, the social criticisms tell you to be prepared for death, the strange looks in the confectionary aisle tell you your child won't survive, you have done a bad job. When will the dropper fill with the overdose, the syringe with the side effect, when will the tyre shred midway through the journey? You allow their deaths to fill you, you eat and drink it so you are sated by it for that is the only way, to live on it and not go insane with fear that it will happen. As it will, of course, in the end, one day.

23. The evening after the accident we gathered at the hall to take down the banner introducing the proud couple and to undress the tables, and though the name cards had been printed with the date they needed to be stored and re-used as who would *care about the date when the wedding day came and the tables were overflowing with food? Only Aunt Delphine and when didn't she complain?* The hall was cold and smelt of stale bread, bonbonniere and rosemary. I was tired and did not want to help. I felt like there was nothing outside the hall, that we would take down the wedding and eat the wedding food and then enter into the nothingness outside which would be colder still. As the food had been cooked and tables set it seemed to make sense to eat in the hall after the wedding had been dismantled. The hall would still have to be paid for. There were also streamers and balloons that needed to come down and bonbonniere that needed to be moved into the church hall's kitchen cupboard – though all of those were in the end stolen by the students of the Lord's School of Dance that rehearsed there on Tuesdays and Thursdays.

24. The honeymoon to the Whitsundays had been cancelled and the priest was given a donation for the service he did not have to perform but no one had told *Blue Sharp* and they arrived with their three blue guitars and blue drum kit and there was nothing to do except find hooks for their blue pin-striped suit jackets and then to ask them to join us to eat and drink.

25. One of my aunts bemoaned the fact that the hotplates would have to be cleaned again, more air needed for the balloons and then her sister asked how on God's green earth, with their youngest brother in hospital, she could dare to complain. *And in the hall of our Father, with our Sweet Jesus looking down on us, you've got enough hot air to fill a hundred balloons.* The

eldest brother tried to calm them but they accused him of setting an example like Eve had set for Adam – *carousing, drinking, Sweet Lord Charles! That hussy was walking around in a towel in front of the boy* – and told him to keep his head on the work and he threatened them both with a slap if they did not *shut up and bugger off to hell*. The argument then lead to an accusation about five aces in a pack last time they played cards and of money missing from the little tin bank next to the phone and it only stopped when Teresa entered the hall.

32. My son is running ahead of me though he should be running behind, throwing grass seed all over the earth we have just dug and watered. He has long brown hair and is often mistaken for a girl. His face is soft. His hair is wet from where he has *made rain* and showered us both with the hose. The earth is dark and puddled and in my mind's eye, as he runs and throws seed, I see the red brick wall in our backyard collapse to reveal the lounge room of my grandfather's house, lit blue by the TV screen on a dark afternoon some years ago – all the dark afternoons, all the years – and I see my uncles. I see them all in that moment, the living and the dead, my mother's brothers, one rich, the others poor from the day's racing – the good bets and the bad, the winnings or savings now invested on the eighth race, cigarettes lit, betting slips paper-clipped at the start of the day in the correct running order – on the nose or quadrellas or trifectas. Then the red light, racing. The track is *dead 5* and the afternoon has shifted and multiplied, the luck cursed then beloved then cursed again. They could not all win and the winner might shout whisky and pizza but not share winnings. *Hang in, hang in….Gone too far from home…get up, get up…* – the ash trembling, the glasses shaking, the men whipping their own sides – go *Pasiphae (4)*, go *Ring Finger (24)*, go *Castellar (12), c'mon – go*. A year after the last race of the spring carnival Chuck, the eldest would be dead – his heart – but here his quadrella mare sees the gap, makes for it, gets a clear run through. The second eldest's last year was a clean, lucky run to death – a new job at Pilkingtons, another child on the way – electrocuted at work in the third trimester. Birds swoop on seed as the scene spins before me. Horses circle the

punters. Women in silk dresses ascend. Elvis spent his last night of living arranging his socks in seven pairs. The lead horse was a stayer and had been in front all race but it still had a kick. With a hundred to go he had spent the winnings on a pair of suede driving gloves. Then the fast closing gray drew level and the jockey changed whip hands. Elvis cursed and Theo leaned forward – he had the gray, the mare had run her race. Theo, with just enough troubles with the boys at the plant to *not* get the union involved, had all the day's takings on 12, with another operation on the plates in his leg looming. It was a plunge but a risk-free one – all on the nose of the favourite, he never liked trifectas – never believed that luck good or bad actually came in threes – it struck out whenever, came whenever, it had no pattern like the stars had a pattern, luck had no rules like games had rules – he would lose the job, he would find divorce papers, again, sitting in the one chair left in the house the day before his fortieth birthday. Papers in an empty house, how could you see that coming, *you could no more see a blue pattern in black, you could no more talk to your brother in the morning and kiss his dead eyelids at night, what times, good times, bad, sickness, health, go on now go, gone too early.* And *– my own wife, who was she and who had she been and who should I have married –* after all, in the end. Women, slim women, pass before my son's eyes wrapped in towels – he cannot see them – the birds fly away. The judges call for the photo, the wall closes.

Sydney

Sun spangling on a banking wing
Diamond scales flaking the harbour
Skips of glint from the bridge to the tower
To the windless bloom of those concrete sails,
Familiar curves of an old lover
My island home –

Sydney, I grew up with you, I cried in all your alleys,
I drank your streetlamps under the morning,
And tasted coffee on your waking breath
As light grumbled over the Quay,
All those scraping leaves and milk crates and muttering
Night ride vigils, those long black nights
In midnight cafés and Chinese kitchens, smoke and wine
And post-mix orange, fuckless nights in piss-trough pubs
And vodka-spittled inanities on the edge of dance floors,
All to see you naked, to touch the roots that have punched
Deep into the Dreaming, and the human stains
Of life grown from bricks

The slow drift began in '93,
When you outbribed the Chinese, and the
Onomatopoeic release of corks ricocheted round
The ferry; fires cracking like an echo in the sky.
I watched the champagne kiss of strangers
And drank to nothing, and water swayed
Beneath the decks.

You spent six years tarting yourself up
For that night on the world –
I was gone by then, and now I cruise your veins
Like a *flâneur*, fumbling for the pulse I
Could once count in my sleep

The cheap face-lift you fucked the city council for
Is peeling all around me I see a rash
Of unsleeping fluorescence up and down your streets,
The graveyard glare of convenience stores lit
By the tread of a somnambulant light,
I see 'beautified' scars on your pavements
And Olympic junk in bargain dumps
I see cold chrome top bars in your grandparents' buildings
I see a corporate toaster blighting your summer evenings
I see slowly ebbing memories in our favourite cafés

I see tourists coming up the hill from William Street
Mapping out lights with their fingers
'You find this lovely, I find it ugly'.

Possible Worlds

So it was a mistake, you tell me, but my emptied hands
don't follow this logic. They know only the yearning

for the skin of your palms, the way your fingers press flat
against mine in a white lie, the colour of hotel sheets

of my t-shirt clinging to your torso, your legs bare and nothing
but the heft and curve of your shoulder under my arm

in the huddled coil of this embrace. Here desire yields
the nonsense of all explanations, chronologies spinning

awry, and the heat of your thigh is enough. In this world
your body unravelling from my arms is like a small trauma

and the mistake is to let you stand there, to not clutch you
close and conjure the intensity of those lights that soughed

in the trees on that lingering half-remembered walk
through drunken leaves, lamp-posts quivering

from the water, each one lighting a possible world
which the flesh knows cannot be winnowed.

Reading Hopkins

Because of you, for you, I am reading Hopkins
For how your voice wrings his words
From within, no worst than sin — how
This sonnet of God-lashed despair
Grips me, socket to bone, on your tongue
Like an erotic shock, a secular moan. Listen.

I am listing. You have sprung me
You have wrung from me all yearning
For other than you, for all that is not
Your birthmarked flesh, or the pitch of your heart
Which I know roils for me, across our ravished
Hours, like "The Wreck of the Deutschland" roils
On my tongue, right now, clockwise toward the sublime.

Dickinson's Envelope

In the Special Collections archives of Amherst college
a twenty-five year old grad student named Lizzie
ungathers the twine around those famous packets
of folded stationery, inked with lyrics of tremulous insight

her excited breath a reprise of what she assumes
would have been the inhalation of scholars before her
in this silent room. Here is the envelope on the back of which

Emily wrote a fragment of thought which editors thought
could be a lyric. Here is the imprint of a leaf on a letter
once opened by her brother. And here are her own thin fingers
cramped from the pen she has forgotten how to use.
Here she is, gathering threads, a bowerbird in the archives.

She knows Emily was a bluebird, although she has never
heard one sing. She writes poetry too. She knows she is no
Genius! – but she too feels the throb of life
and death, the need for her verses to be alive,

to have breathed. She struggles, more than Emily
ever could have, with that long dark horizon her lines
will never breach, the barrenness of her own breath
as she flounders in quotidian musings on teacups

and friendship, in compilations of abstract nouns
typing thoughts which she can never make her own
straight onto the computer, the screen a palimpsest
the cursor her guillotine.

Imagine if from this envelope slipped
a handwritten recipe for New England bread
its inky presence yearning through the centuries.
Could this be a poem, yet unversified?

Two Quarts Flour – a single Yeast Cake
Water – Blood warm! – and Sugar –
Let the loaf breathe unshriven
On a Syllable – till you spy
The Birds come picking

What if she slipped one of her own imperfect offerings
into that envelope? Would it be discovered, she wonders
to become poem number 1776 in another edition, lineated
to the accent of Emily's singular trill? She writes poetry too.

Perhaps, in years to come, a fevered hoaxology expert would cart
her hard drive, her corroded memory sticks, from a cardboard box
in her sister's attic, to the university's windowless IT room
in search of missing drafts. Would trawl her emails

to her graduate advisor, to her family in Australia
google her posts on poetry blogs, her Facebook blurts, in search
of a philosophy, a lesbian lover, a poem that might
have been, before her digital trail evaporates

in the vacuum of cyberspace, where no one can hear you scream.
Maybe then someone would know that she breathed
that once she was alive, aching for a line of flight
from Dickinson's envelope into the clear blue of birdsong.

from Thanks for the Poems, Pauline Hanson

Central / Redfern / Sydenham/ Tempe / Rockdale / Kogarah
Hurstville
From the top floor of the carriage we watch
Two skinheads, rank with beer, suspenders
Dangling from jeans, enter
The vestibule / one sits next to the Korean youth
Pressed in the corner / the other sits opposite
A friendly chat ensues:
'Why you reading that book? / Why don't you read it in English? /
What does it say? / What's that book? / Where you from /
Here, shake my hand / Come on / Don't be rude /
You call that a handshake / mate, if we were in a pub /
And you shook my hand like that / I'd take you out the back
And beat the shit outta ya / shake my fuckin' HAND'
Pumping adrenalin through his hand, pumping blood in my heart
'Leave him alone,' says my girlfriend
He turns, we have moved from the top floor to the vestibule,
What are we, some sort of fucking guardian angels?

He sees her, blue-eyed, fair-haired / he sees me
Black-haired, scowling, trying to fill out
My oversized leather jacket
He makes some kind of connection in his buzzing
Head, draws up to his full runtish height, smirk/snarls
With knowing contempt, with that oh my god / what have we here
– if only he knew, she was a Jew –
He stares, like Hando in *Romper Stomper*
'I'm just having a friendly chat / trying to shake his hand'
'He doesn't want to / you're harassing him'
'He's just having a conversation' says Hando's friend
There's a bristle in the vestibule
Sydenham / Tempe / Rockdale
Two stops to Hurstville
'Come on mate,' says Hando's friend, 'it's not worth it'
It stirs him up
'I'm an AUSTRALIAN. I won't be told what to do
IN MY OWN COUNTRY'
This is not high school taunting of difference
Four-eyed / fat / ugly / nerdy / pimply / chingchong / wog
This is relaxed and comfortable
Kogarah / the Korean has disembarked
I dream of being strong, not for politics, or tolerance,
Or freedom, or multiculturalism
For masculine pride, for testosterone / I'm ready
To cut my fingers on his teeth, to feel his nose crunch
Under my knuckles, his head splinter
Against the window / I'm ready
To get a knife stuck in my gut
For MY COUNTRY, not his
Hurstville / we disembark / my feet on automatic pilot
Twenty years of stepping onto the platform,
Of going home

Done

i

We chose Australia —
stable government,
salubrious climate,
wide open spaces,
and nearness to Asia.

Plus the only job offer
we couldn't refuse — a way out
of the mess, out of the land
of big-time prophets and midwives
who didn't deliver.

And if we had to keep alive
the memory of a broken past,
we could always visit Singapore,
the safest, nearest, when all else,
look up a friend, a relative.

ii

With distance and hindsight,
looking back and forth,
I have no doubt

Our decision to leave
was a correct one;
we had no choice.

My wife and children
assure me they are happy;
we are not alone.

There's plenty of land here,
and meat, fruit, vegetable, wine
and beer – Canaan and cornucopia.

But more than these – a refuge
where we may pause to think, to make
a future for another age.

Resolution

Here, halfway up the Swan, I chose
to build my house, for the last time,
having to come to terms with my new home.

The river pushes on regardless; I am
constrained to check, change the course,
seek other outlets in a boundless sea.

Where is that estuary for my dreams?
How should I merge with the landscape,
melt in a neutral, all-embracing flow?

That mortal day – a flooded cavern, the
struggle, cascading downtunnel, downstream
through forest, hidden valley – I swam
naked into the shock and glare of being.

At a singing lesson in a small classroom –
hey diddle diddle, the cat and the fiddle –
the sky turned radiant, a fireworks of

golden and silvery stars. As now all over
the cow jumps over the moon,
again old words resume, fly into view,

plunge, float, define more sharply — pelican,
cormorant, water-fowl, long-legged bird
white as Siberian snow, winter immigrant.

Requiem

Date from this day onwards
Whatever you will,
Use the momentous day
As it suits you, but with reverence
As befits the great divide.

Tell your children to remember
The lesson of May 13,
Or tell them to forget
The friends and relatives who died,
It makes no difference.

Sun and moon will rise tomorrow
Sun and moon will set

For all our sorrow.

Perth

The city has no centre, focal landmark.
no Place de la Concorde, Padang Merdeka, Tien An Men,
no particular square, terrace, public park.

On important days citizens do not converge,
as elsewhere, for a common purpose — they feel
no urge to (there's no compulsion);

would rather windsurf, sprawl on beach, go bush,
or some place else, even overseas (if it's
not too far, not too expensive).

Alternatively, might as well stay home,
weed, mow the lawn, try a new recipe, barbecue,
lounge, have a beer, watch tv (*Love you Perth*).

Of course. Or else. Yet sometimes,
for a while, I'd rather be away
from family, neighbours, visiting friends;

be all alone, to daydream, diverge, de-centred,
but no looking back to brood, and not too far ahead,
just the opposite foreshore, Bassendean.

And the Swan, quiet, deathly pale at evening.

For My Son

One bright auspicious hour
You will hear your elders speak
Of Freedom soaring in the sky,
And hovering on a cloud, and stirring
In the leaves of sun-aspiring branches.
Inspired, you will burn in your passion
To hack through treacherous swamps
And the darkly creeping *blukar* of oppression.

One quiet evening you will return
To join your elders speaking
Of Freedom hanging in the sky, and
Inspired, you will relate on wings
Of such eloquence the burden of a dream

That your children, discontented,
Will take up your theme,
And seek their godhead, feel their age.

So it will go on and on,
The flame, the smoulder and the ash,
Clearing after patient clearing,
As you cut and criss-cross
Every hydra creeper of the mind
Obscuring caves and corners
Of an elusive wind.

Some New Perspectives

Race, language, religion, birthplace —
the categories do not satisfy:
what do they say of you and me,
the space, the silences between?

Not always negative, I am
more or less than your images,
the truth is always partly,
a few hints here and there.

That's how it is — conceptual
smithereens, in spurts
and starts, a world view,
the twentieth century's, ours.

On Becoming an Intellectual

"You have lost your Third World touch"
He said when I talked of Derrida and Foucault.

He thought they were Tamil Terrorists;
Then I explained.
He said:

"Be pragmatic,
Look for simplicity;
Philosophy is dead and nutty.
Literature doesn't make you rich!
Try to improve on your accent and
Consider doing an MBA."

He showed me the key
To his brand new car.
I walked to the station.

White Mask

Under
A sixty year old gumtree
A plaque remembers
An unknown soldier
In Kings Park.
He sits and scribbles poetry
In English.
Burying
Two thousand and five hundred years
Of metaphors, images
Metre and rhyme now
Heard only at night
In dreams of Sinhala verse.

Summer in Perth

Long hot summer days
Born again
Like bad karma,
Grow with heat and
Live with heat,
Unconquered
By conditioned air.

Paralysed by heat
I hide in a room
Tucked away from this world.

Seeking refuge in a cold shower
Brings streams of warm water instead.
Oh, for my village
Bathing well
Under the *kumbuk* tree
Behind the hedges
At the edge of our paddy field.

Pettah Market

Away from the world's markets
You wake up to another day of
Covered faces,
Fresh vegetables,
Fish blood and
The occasional bomb.

Fremantle Beach

As the sun dives
Into the mute Indian Ocean,
Across the western edge
A dim rainbow fades
Into a blue sky
Painted rusted red.

Sea waves carry
Their ivory froth to shore,
Melting into memory;
Another faded love.

The evening breeze
Whispers over the ocean
Your sweet lullaby.

My heart aches;
No song to stop the waves.

A Veteran Talking

We tossed them high into the air
And caught them coming down,
Sliding straight through
The tips of our bayonets.
Babies cry in any case,
But the women, oh, the women,
They made such a racket;
Had to quieten them down:
That was more bayonet practice.

We had our instructions, we had to clear the place.
We got rid of the men first, one way or another.
As for the women, we did our manly thing with them first,
Anywhere, behind doorways, in the middle of the streets,
Anytime, morning, afternoon, night,
Then we got rid of them, just as efficiently.

It took only a few days
For us to get into a routine.

We did what had to be done:
Shooting, knifing, hanging, burning,
Whatever was necessary to keep order
In a disorderly city.

After about eight weeks
We succeeded in quelling the ruckus.
It was much hard work:
Unending vigilance and continual practice.
Finally the city surrendered.
It was slightly more manageable, for by then
We had cut the population by half or more.

Even so, there was no letting up
For us the Occupying Force.
Unswervingly, we had to keep out cogs oiled,
Our tanks running, our dignity unsoiled.

(Homage to Iris Chang, author of *The Rape Of Nanking*, 1997, with much
sadness at her early death.)

Incense Tree
Aquilaria Sinensis

Incense root incense fruit
Incense loading at the port:
Groves of incense trees
Lined the harbour once
At Aberdeen.

Joss sticks, agarwood, potions, scents,
Thriving commerce
Export trade
That once was,
Gave "Hong Kong" its name:
Incense Port, and its fame.

Truly fragrant truly harbour,
But not the
Exoticised "fragrant harbour":
Incense Port its true name.

Heung not Hong
Gong not Kong;
In any case
Transliteration into English sounds
Of monosyllabic tonal Chinese

Is alchemy in reverse
Changing all that is gold
Into dross, loss and mockery.

Poachers come on hacking sprees
From China with saws, axes and carts,
Depleting our incense trees
That did thrive in these parts.
Aquilaria Sinensis
The Chinese Incense Tree
Is to-day endangered species.

Party

Robotic filings stream down
Shimmering parallel lines
Dusting the estate agent's torso
A Brisbane engineer thinks
Strangely that "story Bridge" there
Has something to do with English Studies
One "Bob" decided to hold forth
About Shakespeare's "importance"
For being "four hundred years old"
Thus the unschooled small businessman bardologises
The pretty blond sitting next to him
Slithering in all directions
Among her non sequiturs
Tried progressively to nudge closer
In the course of the evening

The Other Day

The other day
I used a sledgehammer
To kill an ant.

This happens
Living here
In these parts

Sun scorched land lost
Purblind
I lose
My cardinal points

Where are the tonalities
Of modified colours
Where are the varied palettes
Of older societies

Ad hoc Australia
Has somersaulted
Over two hundred years
It can only look forward

Those strong of arm
Heart and mind
Will nonetheless garner
The dew of civility
From raw hide

The Rains (1)

For three days and nights
the clouds have come and gone without bringing a drop.

I have walked from house to house,
room to room, window to window, and felt you walk behind me

like a bewitched deer.
O when shall you come, my love, and kiss my neck,

lift the round floppy bun of hair,
and whisper in my ear moist lusty groan?

It's silly of me but I wait for you
to paint the yellow sticky mud on my body

and summon four white elephants,
their trunks heavy with water smelling of lotuses and lilies,

to roar tumble and rain like four
lover-clouds, each of them you, and yet different.

The Rains (2)

Two elephants are playing
in the pond and two dark clouds in the sky.

In between the pond and the sky
I like the moist air, thick, heavy, languid and translucent.

Two elephants are playing in my body
one you and the other the insatiable desire.

The first jumps out of the pond and raising
her trunk rains showers on the muddied wrinkles of the other,

after which they change places,
the showered and the showerer, the lover and the loved.

Two elephants are dreaming
in my dream and the rain falls in my sleep and outside.

The night is wet and my bed empty
waiting in vain for you to come and rain.

The Rains (3)

No this is not the rain I am waiting for
but the one that wets my every inner fold.

Don't hold me like this
when you aren't with me but, sitting under some shady fig,

are lost in the realm of the thoughtless-ness.
The *Kheer* in the golden bowl which Sujata, the young girl,

would one morning bring would be sweet,
because the water with which it would be cooked would be me

you have, I know, renounced me and the world,
in order to listen to the celestial rain that showers

on the landscape of your thoughts,
but the foolish thought which warms my heart

tells me that It is me, your Gopa, who flows in you,
and like the rain, feeds your body, thought and soul.

The Rains (5)

The rain has stopped
and the sun looking through the clouds enters my body,

moist and hot, like you, my elephant man, my lover.
Don't make love to me when it rains, I ask you often,

although you know that when it rains
I always wait for you to come, grab me and lift my sari and

from the back enter like a cloud.
And in the evening when I go out looking for Rahul,

my friends enchanted by my
elephant-like walk and the chime of silver anklets stop

and ask me: O look how you glow!
Tell us please what has taken you over? In reply

I smile and they know that the cloud-elephant
which carried water from the honey-filled sea has emptied into me.

The Rains (6)

I come out on the roof
to hear the rain at night and to watch the wet moon,

but the moon has absconded
and the sky, loaded with dark heavy clouds,

splinters into flashes of crimson and yellow
and bursts like a pomegranate.

I hear thunder roll through the sky like a herd
of baby elephants trumpeting through the fields of sugarcane,

when the fire starts, first as a spark,
and then flares up reaching the canopy of wet leafy trees,

and suddenly the shower begins.
Drops like warm crusty walnuts hit my body stretched on the floor.

What's that, I ask myself, which makes
the ache and the grief so sensuous and pleasing?

The Empty Table

I have
cleaned up my table
and soon I shall go
& step outside into
the yellow but wet & cold autumn.

No poem
will be written
at this table
no letter to friends composed
the paper will remain silent
will not call, ask and lure.

The empty table
will no longer be the table:
a table and yet not a table.

O Rilke!
now I walk
instead of writing

and talk in prose
and hunt for bread,
tea & sugar milk & honey
and wait for my son – my Moor –

to come and be there
to sit silently – sullen, unhappy and cross
but to tell that he is there
that I am there
and that all is very difficult
but all is still well.

I am sorry my friend
that you have come into my poems
when life is slowly leaving them
and when all words in my dictionary
have become synonyms of hunger and death.

Autumn (3)

Spring is far away,
but I miss the bitter-sweet taste of *Jamun*,

the Java Plum, of last spring.
You roll the plum in your mouth, suck its brown-purple skin,

press it gently between your teeth
and with a push of the tongue crack it open

to reach the red juicy flesh;
feel its stringy, sweet and spongy hardness, and let it disappear

till the tongue has the pleasure of caressing
the moist warm and striated roundness of the seed.

Don't spit the seed out
but wait till the mouth has accepted the next offering.

Isn't this strange, my love, that even
a small fleshy fruit can tingle such pleasure in the body?

Winter (5)

Do you remember the *Kachnar*
that grew near the pond in our garden?

The one that used to shed
its leaves in winter but always hesitated to blossom.

Suddenly this winter
as if touched by the gracious hand of the blessed one

It has finally
resolved to splash all its colours.

What a luscious opulence of mauve,
magenta and pink! Even the fish in the pond

have lost their way
under the heady fragrance that swoops on you as you walk past.

O shameless, I scold her, why this season,
when it seems the world inside me has turned so blank and dull?

Meena, the Elephant, in the Kabul Zoo

The elephant
on the cover of
Les Murray's *Collected Poems*
reminds me of an elephant
that died last year in the Kabul Zoo.

She was blind
and her knees
and the right back
had cracked.

As she tried
to pull herself up
and lift her beautiful trunk
she swayed like an uprooted tree
and fell down with a thud.

Her head rolled
the ears flapped
and two huge drops
froze near the cusps
of her gluey eyes.

The dust
from the muddy ground rose
and settled slowly
over her parched skin
and spread like dry creeks
through the wrinkled topography of her back.

She was dying
on the hot summer day
far from the jungles of Burma

from where in a goods train
she was brought to a city
designed by a Soviet architect
a student of Le Corbusier.

The chief zoologist
was a communist
who adored animals.

He felt that the children
who had seen only goats, horses and camels,
and occasionally a tiger or a wolf,
would benefit from learning to love the elephants.

They, the children,
called her Meena,
the one with beautiful eyes,
and made her
their princess.

The princess
was sleeping
the night
the bomb
looking for the Talibans
hit the ground
lifting her up like a balloon
and dropping her back
on the dry
lumpy bank of the river.

In the morning
as the hot dusty sun rose
a man on a bicycle arrived
with knife, saw and hammer,
to claim whatever was left of the tusks.

He patted her gently
washed her wounds
and after feeding her
a few lumps of brown sugar
rode away with the loot.

As if
to complete the picture
a girl as young as the one
on the cover of Les Murray's book
walked in the evening.

She fetched
water from the river
flowers from the field
and after taking off
her Jaipuri-legs
sat on the ground
kneeling against the elephant's back.

That is when
I imagine
the man with the camera
decided to shoot.

Possessed

My cousin Fasil might be possessed. The whole family accepts this fact and I am told not to provoke him. An Imam has come to the house to see Fasil and his demonic possession is confirmed. Fasil rants and raves and tells everyone to go to hell, he screams it from the rooftop and refuses to pray, and he spits on the prayer mats and rolls around on the floor laughing. My aunts pray over him. I stay in my room terrified of the Imam.

Ruins

Sparrows find shade in throne rooms, and along balconies at night the goats find beds of soft hay in doorless temples. In tiled bathhouses, in subterranean granaries, in domed towers with steep steps, in cavernous antechambers, a hundred families thrive between walls of flayed silk livid with dye. When their cooking fires are lit, the walls glow like the inside of a blood orange and the pockmarked ruins are best seen from afar. The farmers and goat herders, spice-makers, dyers of wool, asleep in golden bedchambers, asleep for a thousand years, rise to survey their kingdom. Children abandon their families and gather in chambers to plot their transgressions with blackened sticks on rotting walls. They burn the bones of dead birds, pulling at each other's limbs with savage laughter, and for a thousand years they all sleep and wake to find each door open and every golden tower is theirs.

The Onyx Ring

Once, my aunts found themselves the custodians of an onyx ring, the surface of which was polished as black as a dead television set. Inside the ring, a jinn could be summoned to answer questions about the future. The jinn appeared in a human form that was pleasing to the summoner, and I imagined the whole event was like a strange little television show even down to the jinn wearing a fez with a golden tassel. However, the catch was that the person who contacts the jinn must be a child, but what my father was really saying was that the summoner of the jinn had to be a virgin. When I was fifteen I asked my father about the onyx ring, and he said it was long gone. I left home soon after this news.

The Plastic Comb Vendor

He sells only red plastic combs like the dead cigarette girls with trays around their necks at movies. He targets men with greasy hair and rich young girls in groups and asks for a rupee, and the rich young girls wave their hands at him the way people shoo flies. The plastic comb vendor is one amongst a thousand in this city who sells objects people do not want or need. He would be better off selling small handguns that could be concealed in a pocket, or mobile phones, both objects always of value in violent territories.

Veils as Flags

The solution is to dispense with lines. Someone must rub out the demarcation lines that have been painted over valleys and mountains. Or let both sides shoot it out until there is no-one left to fire a gun. Women should refuse to have sex and build a fort on top of a hill and take-up arms to defend their liberty. They should hang their veils as flags and let their hair catch in the wind.

The Land of Smoke

Perhaps my family don't live in the big white house anymore, my cousins don't play handball in the cool shade of the marble archway, and the walls pierced atop with shards of glass have collapsed, and certainly the affluent snapdragons are long dead in the garden beds. The servant's quarters must be dank and their foam beds filled with snails and mildew. Undoubtedly the kitchen is silent with cold ghee and saucepans, my aunts' feet floating above the cool dusty marble floor. I invented the land of my childhood—little girls who look like little boys, and goats that look like skinny old men. Gone are the fresh shipwrecks on Clifton Beach, my cousin Kirin flirting with the ghosts of young boys. There is no more room for people in this land, barely any sky left for kites.

E 44 10 N 33 15

In the year of the Hegira 622, driven from the city and exiled, I arrived at the mountains of the   . The journey was arduous. But I was "armed with the terrors of the sword". And the movement of the heavenly bodies (the western side of the city entirely round) filled the sky. The city was entirely round; the inhabitants remarkable for their treachery. Concerning the treacherous mountains. Concerning the origin of the name "   " (in the palace, there was a small   ). Here the young prince—concealing his deformity with a veil—saw in the heavens the terrible   rising. And "the phantom drew back his veil". Massacred, according to custom, the vast number of the inhabitants. There followed "a grievous famine". (In the eastern sky I saw the sun.) One morning, according to the vast number of oriental historians, the sun "a little after rising, completely lost its light". To the great astonishment of the astronomers, this darkness (in the eastern palace persisting). Persisted until noon.

Voyage

Sullen days. The corsair moves mechanically on its hinges. Beneath our proscenium arch wily ports ply their trade, measuring out the hours in skeletons and lampshades. The hold littered with props. Flat clouds drifting idly along the cardboard coast. (In the dawn they emerge, pale with grief.) I cannot remember biding time in the shallows with the air so steep. And the space behind the sun growing and growing, the stalls silent and empty on quiet nights. There were months when great shadows fell across the waves. And we moved, so it seemed, through lost oceans; past sunken islands from which the sounds of mourning stole. It is true that the flight was exhausting; my eyes reeked of distance. But when the blackness lifted, the horizon— beyond the dim circle of lights—remained featureless, unaltered. Now the shapes of our desires do not change but mimic, with each curtainfall, the appearance of a predictable set of stars. When evening transpires (at the appointed time, in the appointed place), the tide reverses; our loyal machines rise, assemble themselves across the deck. Wolf-like, sand-like. Waiting for that same, slow mirage: the familiar moon, hung from its lamprey sky. Swinging guilt.

South of the water

South of the water, Miss Myra lifts her hoop skirts across a minor abyss in the barroom floor. She sits delicately, whiskey sour in hand, near the window with the air blank and brooding (demoniac?) behind her. Outside the earth churns its muddy music; West Wind blowing, carrying the smell of burning and flesh, knives in the parlour, while an old slave bends to the ground, acutely watching the horizon with his ears. The sound that rises—clear, metallic, far down, down, down but coming up through the damp and the ice and six feet of frozen turnips—it goes: fan blades flicking, saloon doors swinging, ceiling shadows, hand around a drink— Miss Myra, teeth blinking, smiling like a villain.

Two children are threatened by a   , 1924

(Ernst)

"While I was thinking back to my childhood, a vision befell me:" it was a rainy night and the floorboards were "forcing me to look at the floorboards full of marks and scratches" filling with water and "I made a series of drawings". They consisted of a curious collection of "objects". It was 1924. I was at   , near   ,   which had the effect of "a sudden increase in my visionary faculties". It was 1942. It was 1924 and two children were threatened by a   . There was a city in the distance. I did not know its name. The sky was a diminishing shade of blue, diminishing into a city in the distance. I was "carefree, yet full of hope". Beneath me ran the path. Beneath me ran the path that led to   .

But it was 1942. And there was a "third" child ("I was staying at a small hotel by the seaside"). And there was a   on   the roof. I was staying at a small hotel and "Eva, the only one left" was the only one left. It was 1924—the year of the sphinx—it was raining. It held (it was the only one) the child against the fading sky and prepared to   take   flight.

Drowning dream

That August I began to dream of drowning. It was the season of water—strange storms troubled the air. All day I crept along the edges of rooms, avoiding the precious windows—half ajar, propped open with old newspapers—where the green sky pooled. Outside, whole oceans flooded the garden, encroaching on the house and its sagging porch. On the first floor the eaves—swollen, bloated with salt. On the second the mirrors, weeping sodden light; the carpets stained with moisture. On the third I studied the ceiling for cracks through which the rain might bloom. The attic and the landing damp. The skirting and the sideboards. The clocks. Only once (in the afternoon) I moved down to the basement, where a man—quiet and still as a mouse—floated face-down in the dark. Above us, the house hummed like a machine.

Winter

It was not for this that we awoke. Stark trees, yes, and the hour of your coming it was. Like lightning through the grove. It was but a slaughter of bees travelling fast. Travelling still. And beyond the hill Mother England—fighting on her ship at sea. Our homeward vessel moored and bound. Harder and greener and further away the land. Slower the tides. The brackish water. The too-long winter. Nested into itself the coming spring. Travelling slow. Swallows and dying and a flight into stillness we go. We go. Into the pilgrim light. With a frame of bones to mark. The edge of the sky from time.

How to Grow Feet of Golden Lotus

A mother cannot love her daughter
and her daughter's feet at the same time

— Old Chinese saying

1.
Begin with a girl of five:
her arches will be firm
but she will not yet know real pain.
Soak feet in warm water and herbs.
Massage. This will be their last
pleasure, though recalled
with bitterness.

2.
Curl four toes
under the sole like a row
of sparrows sheltering under a ledge.
Bind with a long strip of cotton
or silk — whichever you can afford.
But leave the big toe free:
this will be her keel,
for balance.

3.
Pull tightly
as on the reigns of a disobedient horse.
Time will break them.
Strive to make toe kiss heel.

4.
Every second day turn
your ears to stone. Unwrap
the bandage and ignore

her crying as you re-bind them,
each time tighter. Remind yourself,
as your own mother did,
that there is no such thing as a truly
liberated foot.

5.
Beware three terrible blooms:
ulcer, gangrene and necrosis.
They are insidious as a woman's curse.
A toenail can take root in the sole
and left unwatched, the cleft
between ball and heel
nurses all kinds of enemies.

6.
Two years will train them
into pale lotus bulbs
of the most sensual beauty:
iron, silver or gold?

7.
When she is older
the mere sight of them
peeping from beneath a gown
will arouse in men
the most powerful kind of desire:
lust combined with pity.

She will walk
the walk of a beautiful woman.

8.
The smell she may live with
for the rest of her life.
But she will learn the art of beautiful
concealment: washed stockings,
draped hems, and hours
stitching shoes
of the most delicate embroidery.

9.
A woman with lotus feet
steps through mirrored days
of privilege, sits
under willow trees, works
tiny worlds with her thread.

A woman with golden lotus feet
will always be waited upon.
There are just two things
she must never forget:

Always wash the feet in private.
Always wear slippers in bed.

*The binding process lasted for approximately 2 years. The lotus or bound foot
was classified as gold, silver or iron according to its final size. A golden lotus
referred to a foot no more than 7.5 cm long and was considered ideal. A silver
lotus measured up to 10 cm, and an iron lotus was anything larger.*

Whale

After you came back from the hospital
and I made you a cup of tea,
you told me at the kitchen table
about the whale that came in your dreams.
How in those moments of near sleep
at the end of a day's continent
it would appear: a single fluke, that pale spume –
the body rising up
to claim you. Next morning
the canals of your ears would be worn out
with whale song. And I knew
you had spent another night
deep under the cold atmospheres,
your body a drifting ear
pitched for echo. You began to practise
techniques of breath-holding. Spent hours
in the bath with a watch, trying to learn
back that mammalian reflex: the art
of slowing a heartbeat. Four minutes
left you hauling up empty lungfuls, blood
grinding your temples, the black dots fizzing.
Conversation turned foreign: *hypoxia* and *apnea*
replaced *tired* and *wish*
as though overnight someone had switched
your currency of speech. You told how
under the ocean's pressure
the lungs of a diver compress to walnuts
that expand slowly back: small trees
blooming in the chest. And how,
if a man goes deep enough, the urge to breathe
disappears. You hoarded these odd facts,
cherished them as if they offered
small salvations of the body.

But tonight you are silent, staying up late
again. I hover in the kitchen –
you sit in the lounge, watch documentaries
on television: volume low, the blue light
flickering, counting down the hours
till we breach this world.

The Vampire Squid

Vampyroteuthis infernalis

Literally, from hell. Belling the vast dark
with a cape of rusted tentacles. Dante
drifting red-eyed through the underworld,
propelled by the blue blood of his own
strange order. Weak-muscled yet gelatinous
inventor. When attacked inverts his body
inside out: confusing detractors with the lit
lures of his regenerating arm tips. Scribbling
the abyss with a witchy filament spiralled
down from the ancestral mollusc. When unloved,
conjures a sticky blue cloud of glow-thought.
Expert in mistaken identity: exiled from families
of octopus and squid. Like all elusive creatures –
maligned, misunderstood.

Thoughts of Bamboo

for Michael

Tender yellow shoot in a soup,
sturdy green thicket. In all your forms,
you are my metaphor for love.

Holding fast to the steepest slope
like a mountain goat, slicked by warm rains,
a forest of your graceful scaffolding
slows summer heat green.

You are elemental: sustained on nothing
but clean water and light. Those perfect
spears of leaves seem designed
for practicing brush strokes,
while your stem's geometry echoes
finger bone, spine and fuselage
of dragonfly. Are you evolved ahead of your time
or the remnant of some ancient forest
that slipped uncultivated
through the centuries?

Growing in my backyard,
down by the fence, you generate
your own climate
of mosquitoes and cool dirt.

One morning, when my lover left,
I took an axe to you.
Even with my full weight hurled,
you hardly shuddered before
settling in Zen repose. That was when
I learned the frustrations
of your woody heart, your helter-skelter
of pale roots. Even now, I cannot
comprehend how you can be
so resilient: your empty air-filled chambers
splitting even concrete.

Meeting the Owl

You see through me
instantly, melting
away branches, shadow.
Meanwhile you wear
that primitive mask:
as if shocked to the bone.
It's a floating art
you practice, levering
a binary face
silently over fields,
between gaps in the trees.
And when you call,
a hollowness enters
all things: empty receptacles.
Night is a long tendon
you tear through.
Snow, your pretty accomplice.
When you met me
from behind, all I felt
was a regular wind,
how the world grew small
and for the first time
I noticed the moon.

Bodies of Pompeii

It is not the delicate detail, for the cast is too crude
for that: this girl's face obliterated by weeping plaster,

a man's extremities reduced to rounded stumps. It is
the large arrested gesture that tells these bodies, saying:

so this is the shape of death. Familiar lovers fastened
on a stone bed (whereas life might have ripped them apart),

a dog's high-pitched contortion, an entire family sleeping,
the baby rolled absently from its mother.

Unburied, they weigh more than bone ever could.
They have shaken off the ash and refuse to rest. So many

stopped limbs. Mouth holes, eye holes, a balled fist.
But in the end, this is what halts you: how a young woman sits

knees drawn up to her chest, hands covering eyes.
How a child's body folds, alone at the final moment –

and a man rises from his bed, as if waking for the first time.

Home

1. One Day I Will Find It

I'll follow the smell of food: fried ikan bilis, roast lamb, mangoes;
or the sound of water touching down on sand, stones, mud.
Perhaps the code for entry will be in braille
and I must stand in a dark room at midnight, weeping
and running my fingers over two stone tablets.
It will be in my mouth – a thin wafer of honey,
the bitter salt taste of my husband's sweat.
I will see it, I'm sure, yellow as wattle in winter
and brown as the grass under snow.

It will be a skyscraper, fifty storeys tall.
It will be the smallest, most picturesque cottage.
I will live there alone and with everyone I love.

No children are raped there.
No one eats while others go hungry.
No lying awake, wondering which woman or child
in what sweatshop has made these pyjamas I wear,
or the sheets on the bed, or the rug on the floor.
I will not have to lock the door.

2. Without Warning

An explosion of light. A word that is itself.
A word to possess me. An image so bright and complete
it can only be seen with eyes shut tight. As in prayer.
As in sleep – a dream that outlives reality.
An image to enter me like a knife, like a nail,
hammering in till it finds its reply, taking my body
like breath, like the strong kiss of a bridegroom,
like death, in all its finality.

Someone is at work in me,
translating this corrupt language of my body,
the dark, bitter words of my heart
into the pure language of that other place
where every word is a radiant arrival
that draws me across the threshold
and claims me as its own.

3. A Place to Return To

Bed, toilet, kitchen. Exposed brick walls.
This worn grey carpet, toys all over the floor
reminding me that I have left the life of the mind
for this. "Home!", the children call out in the car,
"We're going home!" They must mean this place.

I consider my father, born into a single room
that housed his whole family. And this –
running water, six sets of taps, a fridge, a washing machine,
enough books for a dowager empress, or medieval king.

If there must be a place, a tent for the body
on this earth, I'll take this one, with the blue plumbago
waving defiantly through the natives, the climbing white jasmine
rampant over the fence, and the mulberry tree, that foreigner
so completely at home, growing taller each year.

Mooncake

Glossy brown pastry
enclosing a red bean or lotus seed paste,
sometimes egg yolks.

Dark street. Tropical city.
Three bobbing candle-lit lanterns.
My father's, my sister's, and mine.

Bright harvest moon.
I lift up my head—
Where is home?

My three year old daughter is sad:
"I am Chinese
but I can't *read* Chinese".

An evil emperor. A virtuous wife
who steals his elixir of immortal life
and floats up to the moon.

My father's version:
"Look, can you see her?
She's feeding her rabbits some lettuce."

Pegging out laundry at night—
could that be the same moon
caught between two pencil pines?

A night like this:
fourteenth century rebels
hide messages in mooncakes—
the Yuan dynasty falls.

Mid-Autumn Festival, 2007.
Armed with fresh gloves
Perth Airport Customs officials
slice open each mooncake.

The man at the fruit shop chides:
"Don't forget to buy lanterns for your children."
He gives me a mooncake.

All of one-quarter Chinese
my children go into the garden.
Who can see rabbits?

White suburban kitchen—
this woman picking
lotus seed paste from her teeth.

Bumboat Cruise on the Singapore River

Rhetoric is what keeps this island afloat.
Singaporean voice with a strong American accent,
barely audible above the drone of the bumboat engine:
"Singaporeans are crazy about their food.
They are especially fond of all-you-can-eat buffets.
Why not do as the locals do and try out one of the buffets
at these hotels along the waterfront." The Swissotel looms.
The Grand Copthorne. The Miramar. All glass
and upward-sweeping architecture. Why not do
as the locals do. Here in this city where conspicuous consumption
is an artform. Where white tourists wearing slippers and singlets
are tolerated in black-tie establishments. Dollars. Sense.

How did I ever live in this place? Sixteen years of my life
afloat in this sea of contradictions, of which I was, equally, one:
half-white, half-Chinese; the taxi-driver cannot decide
if I am a tourist or a local, so he pitches at my husband:
"Everything in Singapore is changing all the time."
Strong gestures. Manic conviction. "This is good.
We are never bored. Sometimes my customers

ask me to take them to a destination, but it is no longer there."
We tighten our grip on two squirming children and pray
that the bumboat tour will exist. Nothing short of a miracle
this small wooden boat which is taking us now past Boat Quay,
in its current incarnation, past the Fullerton Hotel

To the mouth of the Singapore river, where the Merlion
still astonishes: grotesque and beautiful as a gargoyle.
The children begin to chafe at confinement. My daughter wails
above the drone of the engine. There's talk of closing the mouth
of the river. New water supply. There's talk of a casino.
Heated debate in the Cabinet. Old Lee and Young Lee
locked in some Oedipal battle. The swell is bigger out here
in the harbour, slapping up spray against the sides of the boat,
as if it were waves that kept it afloat, this boat,
this island, caught between sinking and swimming,
as I am caught now. As if rhetoric mattered.
As if this place gives me a name for myself.

Like the Autumn Clouds, They are Gone

花样的年华，
　来如春梦不多时，
　去似秋云无觅处。

Only the water now, slapping against
　the sides of the ship as she stands in the stern
　　of the Vyner Brooke and watches China

slipping away, the man with the kerosene lamp
　on the dock, growing small, swallowed up in a maze of lights
　　that recede to a dull red glow upon the horizon and then subside

into night, and so, a whole world slips away in the wash of a ship
  and all the selves she could have been are laid to rest
    in the dust of the city she has lived in. She looks for the girl

who steps out of a library and elbows her way
  through a crowded street.
    She is gone.

Like flowers, the days of my youth —
  they came like the sweet breath of spring
    in my dreams, like the autumn clouds
      they are gone where they cannot be found.

Recycled

Winter's been parched this year.
They're predicting drought like you've not seen
in the last half-century. If it keeps up
the Burrumbeet'll be dry in a couple of years.
The land's bleeding pebbles and salt as it is
and the roos are holing up in town.
Soon the black swan'll be returning to Siberia for good.

North of Basra they're draining the marshes for houseland.
No pebbles though, in Ur country
only salt.
Where will the mythical suhurma go
after five thousand carp years
and GIS.SES, their fish god?

In seaside Brighton
a feathery husband's doing his bit.
Stutters out at dawn with his wheelie bin.
Only at the nature-strip does it hit the poor guy
he's missed this month's collection.
The new steel in his lily shoulders
doesn't dint the salt-wind.

Prophet on Flinders

Walk on the dark side, sister
don't be scared
prophets have walked the earth
for thousands of years
they're among us right now
and one'll appear to see you thru
besides, there's always
the train station for the night.

Last night in Fed square
bombs came down on me
Yeeea, Yeeea – like rain
then the red stones spoke up
Onya mate, keep it movin.
See that yellow V in the tramtracks?
That's my prophet saying, *Victory,*
go for it, man.

My dad had everythin goin
for him – no shock treatments
no needles of any kind, dope neither
only money and a house
'n what does he do?
Lies down in front of a train
and dies. Never gave
his prophet a chance.

Check it out, brother
walk the fine line tonight
'n see if a prophet doesn't
appear to see you thru.

Ghazal to a Qana child

She's asleep, she's dreaming, she's dead still bleeding
caught resting by a tunnel to the hill's rich centre

Beside her, a donkey / an oryx / a griffin — dead or sleeping
or painted, with goat-legs and bee-wings its head is equine

The hill is a matt-finished newsflash
a child and her guardian flattened in its hug

If I had a gift I'd give it to you. Thanks for the water. The
bundle's a grandma slung over a young man's shoulder

The tunnel's the reason the hill is
a target, the toll simply unforseen

Spit in Yudhistra's eye across the night fire and truth hangs
half-born, the rest waits meconium-stained, guise unknown

A car / a plane / a boat — for a telling that honours
the Qanani, I am the chariot rounding the turn

The hill's a hummock pounded like Bamiyan
and I could be pilloried for blasphemy

As I speed away to safety two dust figures rise
thick-thighed gnomes loose-haired to the waist

Bare-bummed to the road they'll wait as long as it takes
for a child and her guardian to wake in the cut red dirt

Night kitchen

She's slipped into my delta rhythm
again, my mother, snuck down
for a quick snack of her favourite
grilled zucchini, rearranging
kitchen cupboards at whim
as she fossicks. Darling, she says,
the triangular highlights
of her cheek-bones sharp against
wisps of smoke curling over
the stove, am I glad to be
down here for a bit. You should

hear the carry-on up there. Dog,
your father said to me the other
day. Dog, I said back, not
about to hold my peace just
because we're part of the one
convoluted mess rather than
two separate. It's alright, no need
to look shocked, just reverse
spelling. Dog, you were always
polite even as a kid. Try it, there's
a glow to the word, a soft
sheen. She's speaking to herself
now. Dog. Tongue-testing
the word like caramel. Dog. They
start off as a wobble in a gyrus,
spread in a faint ripple across
the sulci to seep outside the confines
of her night skull. Two nebulous
dogs above the stove, as the
zucchini chars in my kitchen.

Tiger nights

The moon is sorrow on silver.
In the library of our killings
the bones are mixed up.
Undaunted by history, students
sit on archival boxes eating
burnt toast with organic tomato jam.
The burettes are acid-clean and
ending isn't in the vocab.
Tethered to a rail out the back
I wait his coming, my
striped hunter.

The moon is blood over Vesuvius.
Men watch from the battlements
as I'm marched to a murky
causeway, the women
are in hiding. He swishes
through the night
flaunting his lithe frame
in a lazy mid-air flick, lands soft
on his paws and waits
for his ears to be scratched,
tiger eyes gleaming.

It's new moon at the Sunderbans.
The city-boat's been drifting
for days on the tide, now
in now out, a mausoleum
reeking burnt metal
dead humans and godly
blood. We pounce
on puckish estuarine
shadows, my sisters and I
to pass the hours,
mother's late.

Elegy: Ee Tiang Hong

Flies are thick on treacle in Malacca.
Lizards lug their torsos on an offal
Midden: slammingly the rains slimes over
Verdant sewers. Only vermin rejoice.
I couldn't breathe in the frogspawn, he once said,
To a green acquaintance near Clifford Pier.
The *Queen Anne* swaggered in the harbour,
A hearse swaddled in zebra streamers.
       His loneliness was a soliloquy,
A casual aside I chanced to overhear,
Like hymns overheard through longbows of reeds.
He said little; there's much to say of him:
The wisdom begotten of high injury
And exile. *It broke my life*, he once said;
I feel his words in the marrow of my bone.

A Tropical Babu

for Michael Meehan

Where are those bone-breaking, flesh-tearing days
of fear in the outrigger, of terror
among guava fields? Where are all the brave men
who picked their teeth with the brave bones
of traditional foes, and all their kin?
I cannot endure the serene lagoon,
a simulation of other serene
lagoons lifted from the Gauguin logbook.

And while red salmon writhed in lovos
they packed fresh archives, impregnated us
with mayonnaise fantasies. Ennobled

relics of the European bourgeoisie,
we live out our lives in monthly brochures
and mimic the oaths of most Bougainvilles.

About Aji

I: Roasting

When she stoops, her shade stoops over the wok,
Scooped and gritty and black as grief, to oar
The louring sand like a galley slave, stroke
By alluring stroke, till her being is sore
For that nick in the sky, spelling landfall.
Which, if struck, is no random serendip,
But an art, hot and prescient and visual,
Through which she divines an undulant grief,
Drowning, undrowning her seeded embryos,
That they ripen with suffering, the nuts
Burnt whiskey-bright, crackable as frescos
In age-devoured chapels. These she aborts
With a hod, meshed, cupped like a praying hand,
Straining. Straining for a grief black as sand.

II: Inflating

Why the hem of the bag pressed to his mouth
Recalled earlobes wound around cottage eaves—
This to himself he could explain, yet thought
It odd that the eaves were never just eaves,
But something else always: soft-tummied hills
Reversed by the mirror of a stunned lake;
The humped, shadowy progress of camels;
Teethmark on pears; the webbed feet of a drake;
Or the hem of the bag pressed to his mouth,

A pouting demijohn that hosts a djinn
He expells like some heretical oath,
A physics that swells a world flat as tin,
Which stays a heresy till his hands sow
Belief-nuts—and heresy becomes law.

III: Packing

'Twenty and six to a bag.' Her decree
Was untransgressible, school-teacherish.
So I'd transgress it for a lark, slyly,
Although she'd always know, knowing that risk
And breach were the riff-raff of discovery,
Havockers in whose wake newness enters,
As if by art, with a barnstorming 'I,'
And a roll-call that leaves chaos in tatters.
So they'd sit there in penguin-rows, uptight
Against the enamel basin, squat bears
With smarting ears, like schoolboys nabbed in flight,
Condemned to a mess of soup and prayers,
But who'd err again, whatever the shrine,
For love of oddness, mistrusting design.

IV: Selling

She was fledged in myth: the runaway child
Who left behind a trail of pulsing grain
Then slowly pecked her way back to the fold
To find all as it was and herself strange.
So she'd leave to return to leave again:
The jutesack sin-heavy on the way out
And light as a lack on the back-way in.
Thatch to theatre and reverse. Every night
Trotting up the years with her ambling stick,
When one day, mistaking theatre for thatch,

She fell asleep among the nuts, her cheek
On shells as shells decked a celluloid wretch.
She believed by history she was hexed,
Though all history her story had vexed.

A Wishing Well in Suva

Let the tsunami come,
Let it come as an ogre in grey armature,
His forelocks in the sky.
To this town let it hum
A gravelly tune, and break
In the sound of wind through screes
Over and over and over.
Let it come exactly
At twelve, now or in the future,
When the trader is dealing a lie
To the worker; and the rake
Is drumming a lay on the knees
Of a gazelle who answers to Pavlova;
And the Ratu is consigning
All wilderness to woodchips
Over a hopsy lunch with a lumber
Baron from Malaysia;
And the Colonel is admiring
In a circus mirror his shoulder-pips;
And from his drunken slumber
A tramp is urging the tide to come in
Like scrolls of euthanasia,
Obliterating a lagoon
Where the egret grows sick on toxin.

O but let it come soon.
Let it flower like the 4th of July

And wipe out everything:
Except perhaps a tuft of fern
Adorning some crevice or crack
Where once the tern
Wove a nest from sea-wrack,
And an egg shook the world
(O shook this entire beautiful world)
With an inner knocking.

Dowry

I

Like flocks the dust flew off the timbered hatch
When she sprang the hasp on the dowry chest
And plunged in, elbow-deep, her hand a perch
Swimming in mothballed waters, now a guest
Where once it ran host, rummaging for things
That keep slipping the fingers: a fawn brooch,
A ruched scarf, a blouse raging with sequins;
Until it gleans her wedding saree, scorch-
Ing as that day she left home in a spray
Of pulse and flower, the tears soldering off
Her cheeks and her father looking away,
His eyes drilling holes through a stubborn bluff
Estranging like this stranger, drift-boned, shy,
He handpicked for the apple of his I.

II

Now swatch by torrid swatch, I feel the dream
Unwind in her hands to be wound again
Years down the track by aunts who tack and seam
And smother her girlhood in silk, the skein
Reeling in their present as the past un-
Reels in mine. Amid the insinuating

Chatter, the laughter, I watch her snag on
A doubt, the future a nightmare drifting
Like crockery on a pitiless shelf.
How I want my dumb art to scream, to say:
'Mother, swim out into your doubting self.
Plunge in against the current. Go astray.
I will your life to heave like a Van Gogh
Brushstroke, like verses, like poplar leaves. Go.'

A Bilimbili for Madelaine

Light is glancing off the surf, glancing off
The spick and span ocean of the salver
In which my childhood wavered and went off

To tarzans and tops and to undercover
Cops with smoky eyes and thought-crinkled brows,
Which was the same waver tracking back, never

Letting the tray (weighty as marriage vows
Whispered in crumbling temples and hallways)
Seize on a like-image that could tell hours

And scours divided the weeks from the days.
Wherever I go now, I see my likeness
Lulled in teacups, in dead pools, in green bays—

Except when the light, rid of its harness,
Glances off the surf, glances off the sand
Kingdom in which your childhood is empress

Levying shell tariffs on both sea and land,
Drifting in and out of the haze and draught
To distract with a delicious command

Your master ship-builder plying his craft
In the madder shade of an immortelle,
Who must now draw on a digressive art

To stay your vast impatience, who must tell
Of sirens and fisher-kings, of thatched druas
That swallowed up the sea like muscatel

And retched up our sailor gods, of terrors
That trailed my mad itinerant fathers
To the grail of themselves, to ask: "Who endures?"

Having abjured memories and mothers
They answered with an abjuring silence.
What this hand now gleans and gleaning gathers,

What drives its furious finicky cadence
To lure and lash with liana and legume
Reed flutes fetched up by stormy providence,

Are their anonymities—the fret, fume
And fever of ancestral visitants
Coursing through blood and brain till they become

This reed ark I release to the currents,
To winds that rouse its chambers with a chime,
Bearing your highness and her attendants

(Dryads of the slime and houris sublime)
Out and beyond the swash and buckling roar
Till you're light dilly-dallying out of time

Which I reach for and in reaching restore.

Gran/Nenek

I
There was a time in her
life when grandma would have described
someone of my complexion as
"one of those people."

But now she was determined
to prove to me
"You're not that dark, you know."

She applied makeup
under halogen-
lipstick on pucker,
fake tortoiseshell comb through waves-
-preparing for a lavish dinner,
or a waiting suitor perhaps.

Her world had shrunk and shrunk.

Now the moon
bobbed amongst prescription pills.
Shooting stars scuttled over
unwritten Christmas cards and crackers;
Bottled years washed up
on knitted cardigan shores.
2001 and 1984 and 1944 rolled in on breakers,
shook hands
and sunbaked side by side.

With pearls of cream,
frozen raspberry streaks
on teeth,
her laughter was

certain and intelligent,
while the blooming garden on her nightie

creased,
windblown,
fading.

II
Sloppy segments
of jackfruit,
Pregnant with sweetness,
burning in our bellies for lunch,
then cloudy pieces
of *langsat* to cool the belly afterwards.

Nenek drew infinity
from the folds of her sarong:
hairclips, grubby ringgit notes for younger cousins,
small bottles of burning massage oil —
she said it was made from crushed ants.

O collage of streets she
traversed these years
with bending weight
over shoulders
tapped rubber,
dried fish
and collected trinkets-

I weep and weep
in secret
          rage and rage
at my murmuring phrasebook incompetence
my illiterate smiles

Tetapi—but—*katanya*—she said,
she said with rubbery lips flapping
and lazy eye grinning,
              don't upset yourself- *Jangan susa hati*

Airforce Ones

Nike releases new Airforces today —
October 26.

Blue, clear see-through soles. Tan toned, suede exterior.
Kobe Bryant head and shoulders etched on the side,
Make you look so superior, slip 'em on and just slide.

Some people are addicted to stuff they sniff, pop or inject-
but not me.
I'm addicted to the smell of the patent leather out of the box,
The crisscrossed, immaculate laces.
I criss-cross the world in my twelve and a halfs,
luxurious Swoosh as I'm stamping the pavement.

LUCKY for me, I just got paid. I count it out:
1, 2, 3, 4, 5, 6 fifties.
That's three hundred bucks.
So I break my bread, so I shave my head, so I'm ready to go
BUT
My dad stops me at the door and says
"300 bucks? You should send that to your grandma in Malaysia.
It'd last her for months.
He starts jibbering, jabbering,
Something about how she works for two dollars a day.
He starts drivelling, babbling,
Something about how she's sixty four with poor pay
and

I say "yeah, yeah" and I grit my teeth.
I lace up my ones then I hit the streets.

The dude in Foot Locker has one pair left.
Size twelve and a half.
Man, they're gonna fit so well!
He puts the box in my palms like a treasure chest,
I press it to my vest, grip it tight and get thinking.
Before they were in the box, they were getting packed up in a factory.
Before that, they dyed the hide.
Before that they were moulded the rubber for the soles.
Before that, they had the rubber in a large rectangular vat.
Before that, before that, there was an old lady tapping rubber from a tree,
in a Malaysian jungle somewhere.

And she's working for something like two dollars a day,
And she's something like 64 with poor pay

I look down at my treasure chest, gleaming dully.
Count it out again. 1, 2, 3, 4, 5, 6 fifties.
That's 300 bucks.

I got choices to make.

Queanbeyan

"At 3.00 am, when all the things
Inside the building are still...
The inanimate and animate both
Showing due respect
To the stillness and continuity
Of the outside building matter..."

...I slat my eyes closed, black,
And hear nothing
Besides the occasional gruff tabby or tortoiseshell,
Arching and scrapping beneath street signs.

Yet the town vibrates softly with echoes
Of many things:
Of alcos clustering in the park
Fighting and speaking through their noses,
Crumpling casks of Coolabah.
Or lone widowers, tossing breadcrusts to ducks,
Using the rest for jam sandwiches.
Of highschoolers
Who punch cones behind sheds
In free periods
Then come home and bully over facebook
Or hunch over with gritted teeth,
Masturbating at broadband speed.
Of the leagues club where whores hang after shiftwork
Playing the pokies
Fingers smelling of rollies,
Carpet rich with Jim Beam and Cola.

Of paddocks where we played armies,
Plucked blackberries,
Found used syringes
And hunted for trilobites in shale,
Now levelled for yuppie flats in
Stucco and terracotta.
Of ovals, cold topsoil patterned
By a season's worth of studmarks
And quartered orange peels and
Orange mouthguards.

If you listen,
Further beneath you hear the tinkle
Of types of chilli seeds found nowhere else in Australia,
Carried here in corduroy pants
And between teeth.
Somewhere further down you hear the muttered dreams
Of tribes who once gathered to feast
On Bogong moths where the two rivers meet.

It is a place that breeds disobedience.

A place where you can still sees the stars.

It is possible
To love and hate
A place in equal measure.

A Homeland

I imagined a quiet kiss on the eyelids,
a brown shouldered woman
                              twisting water from her hair.
I imagined hibiscus flowers and wandering rhapsodists,
kampungs full of the wise and noble poor.

These visions stood like icons,
                         preserved in a tranquil, private corridor.

Then I arrived.

I saw Prada and mirror balls,
I saw mosques and malls built from the same bricks,
                         and just as full of faithful.

I saw races dining separately
and skyscrapers as sheer as knives.

Behind walls,
there were half-lit handjobs.
Behind doors,
illegal immigrants traded votes for ID cards.
A protestor called for free elections
while the eyes of moral police cut left to right.

And everywhere modernity churned.

Exile's folly!
Second generationer's hope and despair!
To syphon stories from those who left years ago
                                and then think you understand.

No.
A homeland is a bastard thing,
                a chimera, shapeshifter,
to confuse to enlighten to confuse   to enrich?

Under a dripping awning in Kuala Lumpur,
I see life swell immensely,
                with laughter and chewing mouths.

My eyelids are kissed by sweet air.
I look across the street and
                see a woman wringing water from her hair,

        smiling.

Lightning Over Sandakan

IF this is the last time I see her,
　　　　how joyous
　　　　the falling alphabet of rain.

There is food in our guts,
　　　　laughter spouts from our mouths,
　　　　bones turn to stock
　　　　with *serai* and *kayu manis*
　　　　　　on the old stove top.

Age unknown,
cousins say the years have wearied my grandmother.

But when her eyes turn to me,
　　　　they are keen and bright,
urging me to bear children
and not forget her.

To find in my heart
forgiveness for my father.

　　　　　　Lightning over treetops,
　　　　　　sculpting clouds in flashflare purple-yellow.

　　　　　　　Memory trembles,
　　　　　　　Rain written.

Felda

At first glance, beautiful -
up close, a horror story.

The palm oil plantation.

Green desert,
perfect pattern of oil rich trees,
    minting money.

My guts turn to ash.

There was jungle here once,
        fecund,
loud with orangutan and sunbear,
            gibbon and bulbul.

It has been trampled by the march of days.

My mouth is crammed with big words,
that talk of change but don't ask "how?",
that hide from riddles and catch-22s,
that seep from the corners of my mouth.

He asked,
"why would we care about monkeys in trees
         when our children cannot eat?"

A plot of soil sent three of my cousins to university
who might otherwise have drifted.

So here's a riddle the size of a seed:

      Poor man employed
      Empty plate filled
      Rainforest destroyed

I spit out the window
and wipe my mouth on the corner of a century.

Thursday April 21. Canberra

A raven, half a grove of poplars after wake
one receives news that one is gone
morse calls, toll calls and black
I stand on the ground of the displaced, scything the tufts
dawn bells — mathematical series of grey, and shades
after deaths.
Old People's House washed over with chinawhite fineness
art deco lines and the never-never-mind
a fire, left overnight, burnt to ground, wisps
cataract sky hanging low with a few decoys
one that was my father's ghost
on the mindsets of the villagers, his kin.
Of calligraphy, a word wrested
itself out of the mace of a young monk
wrote itself a wing and pressed hard a final dot
on the floor of the freshly dug grave, soft as flesh —
goodness returns to goodness — lush waves of wild grass rolling.
Under faded clouds, grains of my childhood
now I enter a Greek Orthodox house of worship in Kingston
swim in the rising tongues
of islands and archipelagos and the upturned seas
bathed in a hologram, sun washing over years and feet
held in caring hands, then
cut, roped, shifted, hanged up, nailed, in, out, under, over
dirt — warm, ever so, breathing

For St Kilda Road

A city cut out of paper
country of dysfunctional seagulls
eyes, all eyes, from the housing,
bruised, soft husks
or dire hopeless bells, September
of plane trees
camouflaged & season-drunken,
well and truly
nonentities
beside Mephisto, M in his
tram-attendant's oversized green coat
against a tableau of a Chinese Garden
O stockinged dancers
secretly carrying hearts around
move like ancient figures
on a turning lantern
No, like after
a big flood

They

soon will arrive, knock, on the bluestone slab
utter dropping – signs of excitement
thumping, groping, hidden
blackbirds in mating seasons
stained cranes that had burned into atomic
the whole lot in the fey rain
in the ash, fake
years, eleven exactly, there I was conceived
Saturn had done the gorging, Medea the sub
zeroing in, the falling

of whole house, Kabuki eruptions, knowledge,
namings, christenings, rites of wronging
the other, dedications, mementoes as if
nothing had really

Travel

1.
east of the sea
istanbul three troupes of dogs
go hunting
        outside
a colonnade upended
with bust
        of a commissar
facing billboard of ayatollas
eye to eye

closed corridors, Chinese Quarter, a new year in Cholon
red
of phenomenological texts & struggle pamphlets

deux demis, yin and yang, keep moving
without taking
a position

"that is the trick," you say
among columns of mouths,
red tongued
barking

keep.

2.
ad infinitum
prints
of indian-inked peony
and screen-prints of Mao
with his protruding mole
turning bright red

turning bright red?
shhh
don't question

this is
manu-
factured

3.
after red
black book once more

my name is yellow snow can be jay-blue whitist
you once lived the most agile courtesan
in Nguyen Du's Kieu

oracles and burned fake money
on your grave
books and city gates

barbarian mandarins
turn-coats so hip-
revolutionnaire

dark rooms, trompe l'oeil,
daffodils & tulips
light blue lingerie

we all had a house facing the sun
how it disappeared
before our eyes

the trick of
fire
or its demi-gods

4.
next to a pillow

on tuberose patterned rugs (cigarette-burned and marked)
I am about to

never mind, you say

ice and showers
christmas of hail

leave the money

leave

the dog will bark, a little

keep it minimal

keep

5.

the darkest scent the dogs can't trace
calligraphy, ornamental eyelash
jaywalking below vine-lush balcony
late night quasars, last moons

colonnade of celebrating ghosts, a chord quavers
east once more

Elegy

i.m. poet Le Dat

You count the cows, wrapping up the day
winter up in the barren hills means isolation, that much, and writing
is hard, it keeps sprouting from your head
like fire grass, and you must size up
to those writers who walk in many far & strange cities
who must have dreamed your days and nights
they warm your ears, like a felt hat, figure out your steps, and say
                                        take care
of the lungs, the backbones and the walking shanks;
with them you draw and trace maps
of the future skies, a topology of signs and key words
drugstores and theatres, ports and harbours, and the Presence, youth.
Your lines, scraping against the worn out terrain, draw a contour
shall be back to the house, shall perhaps, if permitted, have a desk
the animals are scything the feed and the mountain stars
run to the low ends of a stream the tribal children
bathe in, their parents keep guard
Water. This, the feverish shout of the first Spring, a rusted key, a
                                        vacuum flask
on parole in a library, you translate texts as a job, live and think

war routine days simply continue from where the hills end
changing of objects in heaven or changing of guards
has less to do with this turning the key, pacing the human walks
on the street there's always a new grammar,
for the immense, the incongruous and the lonely

Fragments of an Evening Walk in Kingsbury

it was a hot evening, windless
the grass
half dead, white with rustling noise underneath
the boy suggested that you go out for a walk
you did
the three of you, walking listlessly towards a park beyond the houses

two women went past us
across the street
their averted eyes and their dog running ahead of them
nose held on a string
elicited from you a comment
about the inapproachability of the such likes
and she agreed by saying that they were all the same
neither worse nor better
being human beings

all the while
the eucalyptus standing tall and dark-green
against a darkness
that was gathering behind the darkened
mute houses
the boy wondered if he could go and sit on the gilded edge
of the bank of cloud and enjoy the sunlight from there
the mother said it was only air
and you the useless
sitting on the wooden fence
watching the cloud change shape
as it always does everywhere in the world

suddenly the silent streets seemed startled
when they heard you say:
i don't like australia
i don't like china, either

the boy's mother paused, then said:
that's right
i don't like china, either
curious isn't it
how beautiful they had thought of australia
before they came here

you watched the cloud turn into a pistol
pointed at you and said with longing:
if only i could have a river here
and stroll along its water and sun filled bank

as you approached your rented home
rank with wilful weeds
you heard your heart echoing an old unpublished line of your own:

how i want to go away
to anywhere else

Spring Festival, 1994

1
even spring festival
does not mean anything to me
any more

having lived 36 of it
in china
it's good for a change here

without the hell-splitting
noise of crackers
without worrying who/m to visit

on the first day
no more reunion
with the family

parents of both sides
brothers and sisters
and the ever growing kids

all gathered for the 30th of the big year
with its food of all varieties
and indefinite length

but here i am
in a house deserted
by a school-attending boy

and a factory-working wife
trying to think of something to do
in a long hot summer

with nothing much to do
when someone called in
and said: it's new year's eve

2
we waited until 10
while it was seven back at home
time they must be watching the seven p.m. news from cctv
then i picked up the phone and dialled the number
001186 713 353007
and i wondered about the wonders of such human achievements
while waiting for it to get through

not without some jamming and confusing and recorded message
my father's voice came struggling over:
i am good
i know you ring to say hello

and i said happy new year
my son said happy new year
my wife said happy new year
until there wasn't much left unsaid
when i thought of something and told father to listen to the next day's
radio australia between 8 and 10 pm beijing time
'cause there would be my recorded message of good new year wishes
to him
and others

3
on the first day of the chinese spring festival
it was as quiet at kingsbury as anywhere else in australia
except for a neighbouring lawn-mower
that was as busy as a bee
buzzing like an incessant fly against the window

my wife had just called the factory to say that she could not go to work
today because she wasn't feeling well
but my son had to go to school
the education system was so horrific in australia
that loss of one day at school
would mean loss of our temper

but i had other things to do
so she was left alone
celebrating the occasion by herself
writing unfinished letters home

[Note: The Western version of Spring Festival is Chinese New Year].

The Double Man

my name is
a crystallisation of two cultures
my surname is china
my given name australia
if i translate that direct into english
my surname becomes australia
my given name china
i do not know what motherland means
i possess two countries
or else
i possess neither
my motherland is my past
my motherland is my present
my past motherland is my past
my present motherland is my present
when i go to china
i say i'm returning to my home country
when i go to australia
i say i'm returning to my home country
wherever i go
it is with a heart tinged in two colours
although there is *han jian* in chinese
there isn't *ao jian* in english
i write in chinese
like australians do in english
our motherlands have one thing in common:
they've both lost M
i have nullified my home
i have set up a home
in two hundred years' time
i shall be the father of the double man

Note: *han jian*: Chinese traitor; *ao jian*: Australian traitor.

Writing a poem, in the sun

The blinding sun of Wuhan, at my East Window
I have been reading like I have never done before
One nostril stuffed, I sip tea from a shadow
The sun is shining on a smoggy lake sandwiched

Between two high rises and behind what looks like a stadium
She puts her hand out towards a tip of my hair:

'It's definitely greyer than before
You left Australia'

In an ancient country one gets ancient quick
One's thoughts slowed down by the futility of even thinking
If there is anything colourful it is the bed linens
That they hang out to sun on the open tops of those high rises
There is an Australian quietness here
Broken only by someone announcing his collecting 2nd hand televisions

'Is the moon walking in the water or is the boat moving between the
lake and the hills
Not knowing where I am, I feel like turning into a deity beyond the
dust'

These words come to my mind facing a world of dust and dusty faces
The sun warming my shoe on the windowsill
An autumn mosquito, dying, is crawling between the patches of the
sun
And the patches of the sun-shadow
My life becoming extremely small at this moment
Turning into this poem and, that's it

New Accents

In Kingsbury, in the late 1990s
The people I met constantly spoke English
With new accents:

P from Wuxi spoke of
Once travelling down a street in Melbourne
I'd never heard of that's called Neechosen Street

C from Canton talked about criminal cases
As if they were crime-mi-nal
And the best contribution he has made to the English

Language was when he said:
When I first arrived in Australia
They tried to fool me around because I couldn't

Speak "Anguish"
What a wonderful Anguish that I've spent all these years
Labouring on, with myself, with my students

Some of them would say "vegee table"
Others would accentuate the "b" in "suBtlety"
And I myself, unashamedly, once pronounced "whore" as "whorl"

Spoke of the "antipodes" like "anti-pode-s"
And lost my M.A. candidacy in Canton
Because I created "ee-Sense" in "essence"

And they, the professors, rightly, lost a genius in me
With their English
And my Anguish

An Identity CV

By and large:	not much of a poem to speak of;
By blood:	han nationality for the last 46 years including this year but uncertain if going further back; there could be some other bloods mixed; a dna test would be needed to determine the purity or percentage of purity;
By birth:	a no hoper, destined to drift for life;
By death:	someone australia will regret to have;
By language:	capable of speaking only two at the moment; bilingual in the sense of bi-sexual or bi-partisan or bigamous or bipolar;
By mistake:	getting caught by two, wanted by none, hated by most, and preferring to be left alone;
By nationality:	australian for the last couple of years; chinese for the first 43; unashamed of either; having a bit of problem with both;
By nature:	a cross-cultural fucker;
By occupation:	a stateless and statusless poet; downward mobile; upward wayward; edgewise, always edgewise;
By race:	hard to define at the moment; some sort of as yet unformulated new theory would be needed;
By skin-colour:	supposedly yellow but looking slightly white in winter or dark in summer if in receipt of too much sun; preferring to be changeable according to weather, and place;
By the way:	i haven't had a decent job for the last 11 years; would you consider taking me on?

The Wounded Butcher

When the butcher, a young apprentice, handed me the change, I was looking less at the coins he was counting out than at the flesh of his palms which were scored and encrusted with dried blood. So many cuts and nicks — I was about to say something, make some witticism or fitting apercu, but I then wondered had he incurred his injuries entirely haplessly, and whether pointing them out might not be a careless, reckless sort of remark — an altogether different kind of injury. I realised I was staring and quickly put my change away, raising my own hand to thank him but I think it was too late, for when his gaze met mine he appeared wounded. At that moment I could not help seeing in his eyes the warm, helpless and fearful eyes of all animals, and it was not far, I confess, from that to the association of the abattoir. Yet I still had to prepare my meal. The kind words of my dinner guests, good friends, entirely pragmatic sort of people, were little consolation, for all the while they were chomping and masticating the korma I had made, I was still contemplating a future of determined vegetarianism.

The Mirror Man

Was shy, retiring, but his problem was he shone and gave a bad impression despite his every effort to go unremarked. He would try to be still, so as not to upset the careful geometry of others' existences, but if he was knocked by the smallest force — a gust of wind, say, or a loud noise — he shimmered and glowed and peopled shouted and raised their fists at him. He would have liked to disappear, and yet he was everywhere, or so it seemed, reverberating and reflecting. At other times he would have liked to speak, to recite a poem, whistle, or even sing, but he was alas imprisoned by an intractable muteness. On certain moonlit evenings, if he became tangentially aware of what it might be to know another, to identify, it nevertheless remained a kind of abstract knowledge, unable to be put to good use. The birds would descend from the trees, catching the coquettish reflections of their bright wings in his silvery glass and then fly up to the sky away from him. No one actually touched him, though beautiful women spoke through him, as though to an ancient oracle, of such things as their longings and dreams. Occasionally, overhearing the cries of neighbourhood children, he was so lonely, so envious of their games and easy camaraderie, the Mirror Man would hope that their ball might crash though and even shatter him – as often happened to a local window.

The Changed Woman

Had she changed, she wondered? For though there were some visible signs of her transformation what was difficult was that the more significant changes had happened inside her and therefore could not really be seen at all. Often she tried to remember and make the gestures of her old self, and while this might have reassured the others, she herself knew this old self was merely a sheath, an elaborate and outmoded disguise. When she discarded it, however, it seemed these people, much beloved by her, could not recognise her and spoke disapprovingly of her new ways. Despite her efforts to win them over, they were unwilling, or else incapable, of understanding her. They went about their lives, faithful to their old habits, while she grew restive and weary of it all, dreaming of circuses and caravans and distant lands. Eventually she devised an escape plan. The heartbreaking thing was she could not say goodbye for if she so much as looked into the eyes of these familiar people, now virtual strangers, she was sure her resolve to leave would itself break forever. So on the appointed day, she rose at dawn, placed a few possessions – heirlooms as she already considered them – in a bag and made her way to the end of the valley and up through the mountain pass. The sky changed, the vegetation changed, but somehow, despite the heavy cloak she wore for protection from the elements, she felt a sure-footed lightheartedness.

Crossroads

Here, at what can only be described as a crossroads, I am aware of needing to make a choice, but hardly know which way to go. If I go that way, then there are many things which may go wrong, which may even be disastrous. My lips tremble and my legs quake and I shrink a little from the unknown territory whose very danger is, I have to admit, also thrilling and inviting. What worries me most is having gone that way, I don't know whether I can then turn back or retrace my steps; don't know if it will be possible to return, with the same relaxed step, the same ease of purpose, as before. Life will be harder after having gone that way, if only because I might discover certain things about myself which until now I have not sought to bring into any careful focus. But the other way, tried and true, also does not satisfy me — perhaps because it is so familiar. In a way, that well-worn path has become so useless that it is a dead end of sorts, and I have often said this to myself, while nevertheless returning, by force of habit, to it. Always arriving at the same place, I cannot but think of that other mysterious route, or destination, which makes my heart leap but which, until I make my way there, will always remain a foreign country, a Xanadu of the mind.

Oriental Lilies

Their lips and many eyelids
Opened overnight like a
Voluptuary of the dark
It was hard to look at them
Because they were so beautiful –
Those whites and dragonfruit pinks and
The tiny raised spots on the inner skin of the tepals –
They put me to shame, asking nothing
Of the morning apart from
The obvious – to be looked at
To be purely and mutely objectified.
Full throated and yet without
The familiar plaints or clamour of desire...
Of course, as the day wore on
The blossoms became more heady
With their signature perfume so that it
Almost saturated the dining room and by
Evening had become quite intoxicating.
The saffron-coloured dust fell little
By little and its tincture stained the
Whitewashed surface of the table.
It hardly mattered; I let it fall, without care,
And remarked how something could be
At once so utterly mortal and ethereal.
On the third day there was no denying
They had begun to brown and furl at the edges;
The two blossoms that had not opened would not now
I somehow knew. Then between conversation with a
Friend one flower just dropped, cascading to the floor,
Indifferent to our words: 'Poetry', 'Art/Life';
'Safety' & 'Catastrophe'.

Healing

The skin where it had
Blistered has now grown over
So that I may abandon the bandages
Though there is still a little rawness where
The heat must have first penetrated and got
To the deeper tissue. It's no longer inflamed, though,
Nor really sore...more of an irritation of which
I'm reminded whenever I shower
Or when the arm moves through the super-
Epidermal layers of a shirtsleeve (though I prefer no
Iron at the moment and regard with new caution
A saucepan, the stove). Somehow, however, I find
Myself unthinkingly making tea, caught in the pleasurable
Abstraction of it all; unconsciously handling the cup,
The jug of just boiled water, the entire ritual in which
Nothing much is invested, the soul at ease; playful,
If not entirely forgetful. Later, the scar happens to reveal itself
Beneath the lamp's quiet glow, yet the mind,
Not needing to go over what the body has already
Begun to attend to – the second skin emerging,
Tougher, inevitably tauter – merely glances
Before moving on toward the page's surer
Radiance, its nimbus of spectacular words.

Father

Confucius once said that a picture is worth a thousand words and those words became clear when father showed me a photo of himself, taken in the summer of 1964. From that moment, the floodgates opened. What first caught my eye were the blown hao mai flowers in the foreground, freckled across his smile. He was pointing towards the horizon, collar of his jacket turned up, looking brave. The Marble Mountains were towering in the background, breaking through a sunset stained with blood. But what stayed with me was the golden military insignia stitched on his left-breast pocket, where I imagine he kept postcards for his loved ones. All of which told the story of a soldier marching along Ho Chi Minh trail, battling a dark jungle, alive with flares and tracer rounds. This made me think, just for a second, he could have been a Vietnam War veteran. Yet my attention was drawn to the refugee boat, captured in the distance, ready to sail through a light calling from an unknown land. I imagine father rowing the blue oar at the halter, hands curling to a fist under its huge jaw. I visualise the storm he rowed through to arrive at our adopted country's harbour. I see gale winds stirring evergreen pines, threading the changing leaves of autumn, promising continuity in a transient world. But amongst all that gossip of words, it was father's hands I remembered the most. They were hard working hands. Hands that bathed children, bandaged cuts, dried tears. Today, his hands are infinite grains of sand, placed beneath our feet by the great and restless ocean.

Mother

I know now, as I did in my childhood wonder
that my mother dreamed of a paradise
one unbound by war and exodus.

On the living room carpet we sit
I pluck her grey hairs and ask:
'Mother, what ever was your passion in life?'
She smiles—that eternal smile
a question suspended in mid-air.
Her neck tilts like a sunflower
too heavy to meet the sky.

Gardening is the reply I expect.
My mind's eye turns to childhood, to shadows
stirring beneath star fruit trees
rows of cherry tomatoes growing over fences
a call to supper while sleeping
amongst lotus-dotted ponds.

'Teaching was my passion,' she says, 'high school.'
I smile in agreement. And as I do
jigsaw-puzzle pieces of memory
lock together, my past made whole.
'A literacy teacher,' I exclaim,
she smiles, remembering with excitement
the moment I arrived home from school
with a certificate of improved literacy.

I continue to pluck her grey hairs
our conversation lingers on
as the soft daylight illuminates us.
I know now, as I did in my childhood wonder
about mother's youth, before the bloodshed in Saigon.

I picture her driving a yellow scooter
on the road to school, the freedom
of her hair, a glimmering smile; spiriting past
street markets, the soothing aromas
of Pho and lychee tea; that familiar
crescendo of rickshaws, bicycles and scooters;
landscapes of water buffalo, ploughing
the flooded paddies from cloud to cloud; each one
picturesque from her classroom window; and all of which
was the city she will no longer call home.

More grey hairs fall, the past realigns itself and
I know now, as I did in my childhood wonder
that the teaching legacy passed down to me—
I knew the responsibilities of providing
for her children outweighed
university-degree teaching aspirations.
That in mind, I tell her:
'Mother, this week I taught my students Wordsworth
saw thousands of daffodils and thought of you.'
She smiles and I'm taken back to a halcyon-time
in childhood when she stitched floral
pyjamas, tablecloths, bedsheets together
using a sewing machine for less than $5 an hour
to afford rice, pork, Asian vegetables
and help pay for my tuition
so I could learn to spell 'persistent' correctly—
praying that I might speak an unbroken English tongue
and never be confined
to the labours of factories.

I know now, as I did in my childhood wonder
what it must've been to mother, there
among the refugee boat's thrum, the faces
of Saigon watching—eyeballs ribboned with flames
incandescent, a disorder of diaspora animate
in the missile storm.

The homeland was a mist, the cerulean
depths of sea stirred on the horizon like some agitated womb
boats wet as one long vowel, as the city crumbled
and my mother among them fled
with nothing but me, growing inside.

Refugee Prayer

When I think about peace
I always think about a calm place
white
awash with sounds
wind lifting dunes
like the curls of a fossil
somewhere
where the gun does not point at my father
and me
nor beats my mother
I remember the day Communist soldiers stole
her wedding ring
tossed it on the ground
where the red opal stirs memory
bleeding this changeling to madness
somewhere
where there is no machine gun rattle
as mother tucks me in bed
while she whispers a prayer
for an island across the sea

away from this rubble of a country
lying awake on the refugee boat
listening to the vast ocean
making conversation
peace
    peace
        peace

Fall of Saigon

After the paddies rose to attract a murder of crows—
after the kapok forests were bombed away,
after the earthworms became leeches—

the Hue women were raped
in passing; the Da Nang children
were dragged into tunnels dark

to have their brains thrashed out;
the Saigon men had their throats cut
to coat the Communist flag,

then had their scrotums torn
for tobacco pouches, and then exodus
fled to foreign continents, as far away as peace.

Mr Wong's Children

we learned how
not to stand out
from insults what
not to wear

we waited for
silence to tell
us that we
were good students

though speaking
with no accent
was as easy
as water the eyes
were a little
hard to hide

Resonance

I.
My aunt's family in California
called with the news
the day after the funeral.

Sick for six months she'd
left specific instructions
to tell us after the fact.

They'd waste their money,
she told them, *to fly down here.*
They believed her.

I picture the shock on father's face
eyes unable to focus
on the surrounding room.

Perhaps it was shaking
perhaps it was the endnote
of a tremor arriving from far away.

They say here on the west coast
we are due for a major quake
in the next half-century.

Buildings will crumble in ash
pavement crack like glass
we could all fall into the sea.

Somewhere, a bell rings
its resonance travels towards us.
We believe it. We do not believe it.

II.
These days I see them I forget.

Chinese school after regular lessons every day
then turns at store counter, weekends longer
or driving eighteen-wheelers full of produce.

Bear claws, when found, would mysteriously appear
wrapped in newspaper, be treasured
and transformed to precious healing soup.

Medicine of tree bark, roots, unnamed animals
tasted bitter as expectations. Or worse, as shame.

All of my father's siblings: as different
from each other as a hand is to an eye
but still, brothers and sisters.

None of their old medicines saved her
and father now has lost another of his pieces
without a chance to grieve
in the style of our generation
with its caskets and processions.

As for old ways, we have no altar
in our house to burn incense for the dead
nowhere to place oranges to provide sustenance
for the long journey to the other side
or to give them sweet earthly remembrance
as they watch us from new hidden places.

As for me, fascinated by mirrors
but frightened of damage
by unforeseen circumstances
(a wall shaking, a crack that forms).

I am of no use or comfort
this would-be poet son
who has taken so few opportunities
to ask: Father
tell me about the old days.

Quiet and Odd

Darren Lee and I were superstars, unafraid to swing
from the highest branch of his backyard's gnarled
apple tree, we terrorized insects, older
high-school kids, made snarky remarks about

Mrs. Kopinski in the corner house simply because
we could. We sang: *Jesus Christ /*
Superstar / Who in the hell do you think you are.

'What a shame,' adults told us. We couldn't speak
our ancestral language. Nor could our mothers! Tell
them they've lost *their* heritage. What's the use anyway
of those clattery loud towers of nine tones, building
blocks flung at you in too-bright colours?

Besides, we were not Bennett Ho whose mother
banned him from sex-education class, not Adrian
Tong with his rice-bowl haircut (the fringe swinging
round his head like a carousel of animals). Brian Tom
not yet into his teens expected only bad things in life
so as never to be disappointed. Not Jacob Chiu
whose Mom shaved his skull, everyone wanted to
feel its tiny combs against their fingers. Dominic
Kong was certainly not us, he told people he didn't
know Chinese but who could follow his broken
English? Definitely not Joseph Fong who stepped
in dog poop and didn't care, the playground
suddenly the Titanic sinking, passengers wailed
ABANDON SHIP!
                            It wasn't just that they were odd.
They were quiet boys. Not like us, nails on chalk
boards, fire drill alarms: when my voice broke
I couldn't even whisper without getting in trouble.
We reckoned their tongues got caught on the way
out of their mouths like jackets on doorknobs
as they rushed outside, their mothers calling them
back to do their homework, mind their grandmothers,
though even they'd pretend they couldn't hear
or understand whatever language shouted after them.

The Leg Crosser

Don't cross your legs like a woman!

A man's right-angled knee
is what money is made of
the outer bump of the ankle
rested across the other leg
and just behind the knee
a wide triangular space
for the testicles to breathe.

A lady's pose would suffocate
the thighs engulfing each other
so bold the forward knee
so wanton the free-kicking foot
you could tip out of balance
with such missing solidity.

> *What happened was prophecy*
> *I tipped over*
> *out of my own masculinity*
> *into schoolgirl crushes on other boys.*
>
> *I also crossed my arms incorrectly*
> *like shivering instead of defence*
> *crossed myself profanely in church*
> *and my eyes, when crossed,*
> *frightened rather than amused.*
>
> *When I crossed my delicate fingers*
> *long and toothy and curved like crescent moons*
> *I wished for the unimaginable.*

Is this?

Is this somebody you could trust with your life?
Somebody you could trust? Who you'd leave your
child with? With whom you'd have a child? Who
you'd loan sugar to? Who you could learn something
from? Is this someone whose name you'd forget — after
sleeping with? Is it someone you'd trade seasons with?
Hockey cards? Secrets? With whom you'd share a
grimace and swallow a flaming sword? Who has similar
canine teeth? Someone you'd go on vacation with? Turn
your back on? Leave when they shed tears of repentance
and grace? Someone you'd call home? Someone who
reminds you of someone else? Someone to talk about?
Is this someone you could take advice from? Who you'd
take seriously? Who you'd swing by the arms and not
fear for gravity? Who considers the stars? Who eschews
maps? Who prefers solids to liquids? Is it someone who
remains tangled? A person who cried wolf? The one who
said the truth? Who ate the last biscuit? Somebody you'd
walk to? Someone worth hitchhiking for? Someone you'd
buy a ticket to? A person you'd buy passage for? Someone
who brought you back? Who gave you what you never
thought you'd have? Who polished your shoes and darned
your socks? Who never really knew you except for your
tracks in the sand? Who always thought you shady? Who
you introduced to your family? Who you'd invite to your
funeral? Who forgave you without reason? Is this someone
who depends on more than circumstance? Who left you
feeling tried? Whose habits rubbed off on you and will
never disappear? Is this somebody who could make
redemption feel like a usual state? Is this somebody?

Ranjith Singh's School Days

Ranjith wants to be
A blonde bikie hunk
To impress the chicks
Like Murphy the surfie spunk

Ranjith is not Kathy's type
But she is curious
To find out
What he is like

Ranjith and Kathy
Fuck in silence after school
He's no different
Just like the other dudes

Same adolescent eagerness
To get it over with
First to come
In order to go

Ranjith you've got great skin
Wish I had a tan like you
But what'll Kylie and Debbie think
Me bonking the only darkie in school

The Kadalay Woman

I walk in the sweltering heat to school
wearing a uniform designed for temperate conditions
passing beggars and vendors bare-bodied in sarongs
selling mangoes.

I pass her in the park under the banyan tree
where she sits on her haunches
her mouth red with beetle nut.
She turns her head to her side
like a dancer, revealing her young profile.
She spits a red globule that lands on the dusty pavement.
I ask her how old she is.
She says fourteen.
I say thirteen.
She tells me to buy some chick peas.
I buy some.
I ask her why she is not at school.
With a laugh that reveals her red teeth
she tells me to get fucked.
She points at me, her arm outstretched revealing her rough palm,
telling me she can't afford to, unlike "some people."
I stare at her.
She rolls in laughter slapping the base of the banyan tree
placing her fingers covering her mouth.
She gets ready for another spit,
making that indescribable noise.
She spits a big red beauty in front of me just missing my shoes.
I turn to school, leave her
laughing under the banyan tree.

Note: Kadalay is a Sinhalese word for chick peas.

Immigration Blues

My friend you say
I can never be a revolutionary
because I was born with a silver spoon in my mouth,
never having to fight for my next meal.

You say
I can never really know the freedom fighters in my tropical isle,
as I have never walked bare feet in rice fields in a sarong
carrying stolen shot guns through snake-infested jungles.

You say
I can never know about unsatisfied pangs of hunger,
as my hunger was satisfied at every occasion by opening a fridge door
and grabbing yesterday's curry wrapped in alfoil.

You say
I am not a true child of the Third World,
because I am sipping decaf in Paddington
fascinated by the latest movie made by a Third World director
about slums in a faraway land.

You are wrong my friend
I have been spat on and called "nigger"
during a fight in a pub and was told to go back to the trees where I came
from.
I was told that I speak funny and punched in the face.

I can tell you how it feels to be a child of the Third World.
How I share their pain.
The pain I never felt in the country of my birth.
The pain you forced me to confront.

The Foreigner

Like a little bird, one you've never
seen before, who appears to have accidentally
flown in
       through a slightly open window
       and into an enclosed installation, enlarged
with people busily pecking at their own
and other people's lives – flocking, talking, necking
laughing
       oblivious to what has just
       happened. You've seen it, but you're
paralysed with hopelessness. What can you
do? She's too fast to catch, filled with
moments
       of panic, then stillness. And you watch
       her, realising that now, only seconds later
this furiously flapping bird
once frightened, now seems… okay, quite happy
in fact
       exploring her surrounds, making the most
       of the situation – nibbling at crumbs
jumping around feet, moving along with the crowd
blending in, and it seems that even if you
wanted
       to help her back outside, you may
       frighten her more, and perhaps
even be going against her will, and so
all you can now do is simply watch, slightly
amused
       who's to say she doesn't belong
We all do
       don't we?

Dark skin

I forget I have it, until I remember my childhood
when nearly every student felt they needed
to remind me that I was not of their whiteness

I forget it clothes me, until I leave home
and catch photographic glimpses in bus windows
and *ad hoc* reflections, reminding me

I forget it owns me, until I'm asked where
I'm from, for I can't be from here?
But from somewhere else, a place I don't really
know and that has forever branded me

I forget its beauty, until I see it on other
bodies that carry it with dignity
or when they are clothed to celebrate
their difference

Only one of my many parts, yet mostly, the first
one you'll see when you look at me

I forget, then remember
I own my

dark skin

Ghosts

I missed them
for a while, and thought
I'd forgotten them, but

as I wander
these crowded streets
my mind turns
to   them

    they have yet
    to leave

Each time
I think   they've gone
    their shadows
        fleet past
            on other people's bodies

    They exist, perhaps
    only streets away

    haunting me

I've exorcised
as much
of   their physical presence
as I can

    but those shadows
        re-appear

        entering
        my bloodstream

        chilling me
        viscerally

Chord

One by one the notes are released

Then, as they blur into each other,
there's a moment of dissonance

until

they all fit, perfectly, together
making it easy
to forget that once, all this
did not exist as

one

and just as you sit in this perfect
chord, it moves away and another
begins to form, and you

watch

the harpist's fingers caress the strings
simple movements with transcendent

results

Like a sunset whose beauty cannot be
frozen in time but moves, life
not even just this once, will it stop

pause

And you sigh out this reality

Periwinkle blue

is today's sky, unblemished
by any cotton wool-like clouds
I feel the sun sit gently
on my skin, gently easing
me into this moment
and I surrender to it, dance
with it, not wanting to taint
it with my plans and agenda
where any brash move
could erase the simplicity
of what surrounds me, and now
I think of you, who
always accompanies me in these
moments; and so we recline
into this day, letting it be
our afternoon hammock

Currency Lad

Darwin, four years before I am born
      & your perm
is an informant for Cyclone Tracy.

The way you'd pirouette into an Arnhem bar
      like an exotic cocktail
      no-one's ever thought to order.

Further south you took an Indonesian lover
& left him windswept,
      beguiled by your gyre.

I cannot remember
whether you said he was a
      a) boatperson
      b) philanthropic businessman
        who sold drapery in Glebe or
      c) free-wheeling drug-dealer
        with little other expertise.

This afternoon outside my window
implausible plastic fencing
prevents traipsing on an imported lawn.

The mud is heavy underfoot.
A swift spring wind toots through the court
like an army of tin roofs routed.

Since you left for that place
far beyond Perth,

I've found myself buried
in a study

of swamp drainage
& mosquito birth,

where the harsh susurrus of skulls,
the sough of each gaping eye-socket,
accuses the composite silences of my marsh,

the way loose change shouts
from my otherwise empty pocket.

Mandarin

I separate the seeds from a mandarin
using my tongue and teeth together.
Sun-emblazoned tambourine.

Then consider the endeavour of those
microscopic creatures that must
eat their way out of their own mother.

Or are they blessed who must erase
all trace of their past to gain passage
into this dust?
    They'd never question

whether they discovered enough
before her last, about themselves,
about herself, and the way the world

thought when she was just a tot.
Nor would they remember how
she burst in selfless ecstasy

just as they were done dining.
Perhaps it's the ease with which
I spit these seeds into the bin.

Nothing will come of them.

Arrowtown

The mountains here are never still
        you say, skimming a piece of Otago
schist across the Arrow river,
        the stuff of miners' huts, chimneys.

Making room on my memory card
        I delete surplus macro shots of lichen,
close-ups of metamorphic rock,
        to take snaps on my digital canon

of you by the hawthorn and the rushing water,
        where silver ferns curl like pages
in damp air. Wind in the speargrass
        deposits pollen. We are alluvial.

No time elapses. The newly sharpened light
        sparks a bonfire in your hair —
creatures come scurrying from the char,
        woodmice and wetas. Is that a lens flare

or the red underwing of an alpine kea,
        neophilic clown of the mountain?
A breeze whistles over the quartz reef,
        whipping up whitecaps on Lake Wakatipu.

This was the Ford of Bruinen,
    where the Nazgûl charged Arwen
ferrying Frodo on Asfaloth,
    galloping for safety to Rivendell.

Inventing no new language, we play
    landlords in the abandoned cottages
of migrants from Guangdong,
    miners who panned for li shung,

a chance to dig quick riches: Ah Lum's
    store bustles with gooseberries,
strawberries, ginger and pickled lemon.
    I'm Tin Pan, slinging fresh vegetables

on my bamboo shoulder-pole;
    you're Ah Yeng, whose teas we praise
as tastier than the customary manuka.
    Who then will play the Reverend Don,

converter of fewer than twenty souls?
    Here at the end of Buckingham Street
the last survivor swapped his gold
    for opium and dominoes.

After photographing poppies
    in a purlieu, sluggish after lunch,
you yawn on the path to the cemetery,
    where flecks of mica in a headstone

chime with the lichen. I point.
    I click. I store the crumbs
of light on the pervasive, evershifting
    schist, forgetting the olive plumage

of the kea, the bedlam of blue
    delphiniums. I catch your yawn.
The river swells with whitewater horses,
    douses this blaze of Mesozoic stone.

Recycling Night

By the electric cyan glow of my phone
I swing open the screen
illuminate the snail-silvered path
to the concrete underworld.

Fruit bats chatter in a sweaty club of mango.
I breathe the password
and the golden silkweaver's wasp hoard
parts like a glass-beaded curtain.

Promising to tip the gondolier
I untie my nylon kayak
and kick the pylon, set off at a clip
for the islands of Murano.

When we hit the coast I keep an eye out
for the torchbearer who turns
wine bottles and honey jars
into flutes, chalices, chandeliers.

Then to a deeper circle no echo detects:
the North Pacific Trash Vortex,
where hulls knife swarms of brilliant krill
choking on microplastics.

Stop off at a pontoon of photodegraded
laundry detergent containers;
kneel by the skyblue bic that nests
in the shallow bowels of an albatross carcass.

Returning late, it's there on the edge
of vision, a small form
wrongly still and silent: a noisy miner
static on a branch of coastal oak

overhanging the letterbox.
When I shoo only its eyelid flinches.
Even when I menace with my oar
carving fierce swathes of humid air,

even when I bathe it in my cell,
its features wizen into stone,
the hard seed of its skull taut as a walnut,
a small scoop of clay annealing in a kiln.

Missile

I wake to my machine
unzipping the Sunshine Motorway
at a hundred and fifty.
Arabic numerals bloom on the dash
like bacteria in a petri dish,
lit with firefly luciferin.

In two million years Pioneer 10
will rendezvous with the bullseye:
Aldebaran, patrolling the eastern
horizon, a hundred and fifty times
more luminous than our sun.

To ride this missile to Pleiades,
return with fistfuls of blue
jewels: the trick to finding them
is to avert your vision, look off
to one side, allow a less abused
section of the retina to drink
in the distant emanation.

Circular Breathing

for Samuel Wagan Watson

There's a man with dreadlocks playing the didgeridoo
in the Piazza di Santa Maria, and everyone is listening.
Kids sit by the fountain swapping smokes for laughs,
tourists lick gelati as they pass illicit markets,
belts, handbags, sunglasses, all made in _____,
the place scratched off. Nuns halt, then the Carabinieri,
white gloves, black steel-capped boots glistening.

The crowd hems the young musician in,
faces glazed with wonder: from where could this
strange music have come? Surely not this hemisphere.
A drone as deep as unexcavated ruins, far older
even than the Forum: Armani, Ray-Ban, Dolce
& Gabbana, all sink at once into equivalence.

He doesn't do the kangaroo, the mosquito or
the speeding Holden. Just the one dark warm lush hum,
the clean energy of circular breathing, lungs
and instrument the sum, familiar as the accordion
yet strange, as though not for money, nor just for fun,
but for reasons unknowable — some vast, unhurried Om.

I want to bolt up the stairs of the fountain
and claim that sound as the sound of my home –
but stop when I recall how rarely I slow to hear
the truer player busking in King George Square.
Memory kinks my measured walk into a lurch.
My stomach fills with fire. Far above cold stars wheel
around the spire of Rome's oldest Christian church.

Today

(in the Scottish highlands, early May 1998)

The mist on the hills today
does not resemble the haze
folded over Jakarta.

The fires in the Chinese enclave
hove no relation to the clouds
drifting up from Inverness.
Who can say why
the image of food riots comes
unwelcomed to a kitchen in Teavarran?
The frosted window to my room
would not interest a masked looter
and hot chips from an unfolded newspaper
have smeared an inky oil over
stories of rape in Indonesia.
I find how hard it is to clean
black stains from fingers later.
A family fleeing a burning home
walk up a tussocked slope towards
sounds of laughter coming from
a Scottish farmhouse tonight
only because my pen pushes their
presence to the surface
of this page.

Noodles

"*Eating noodles,*" mother says,
Putting down her coffee cup.
"*...the only thing Chinese about you.*"
I look up from the steaming
bowl of noodles, eyes half-slit
at dawn. Too tired to argue,
I slip into old habits;
an inscrutable smile
and a filial, obedient nod.

Geography

This strange
moment of clarity
when the hum
of a telephone
call between two
continents breaks,
whispers,

"...forget where
you come from..."

– fragments
of my father's
words from
unspeakable depths.
The rattle of hail
against the roof
obliterates
the rest.

from Ancestral Shadows

I'm so tired of writing about
being Chinese as if it were
a loss. I'm a bridge of compact words
lining a page brick to brick,
a wall built on a white sheet of paper –
the colour of mourning.
I'm the professional weeper at the end
of the funeral, crafting teats
for families too numb to cry.
I'm a street sweeper flicking litter
into stormwater drains
smelling of shit. I'm the child
that falls because he's too young
to walk. I'm light suffusing
painted mountains on paper rolls,
edged out of view as if
painting the sun would have polished
the colour from Chinese art.
I'm prosperity and luck
in translation, limited only
by a foreign vocabulary. I'm fire
for ancestral ghosts who walk
in my shade.

And all this is past.
The hollow loss
at the center of a lie,
a middle kingdom which no longer
exists – a fist that spreads
pink and red fingers at dusk
in the eastern sky.

Highlights

(The Migration Museum, Adelaide)

Mostly obvious –
commemorative plates
of Queen Victoria,
grainy photos of refugees
clutching all that embodied them,
a wall of embroidered national flags,
ploughs, tea chests, walking sticks and
passports from many nations
with faded names.

Just before leaving
an exhibit highlighted entry criteria
under White Australia.
An uncomfortably long
pause as I waited for a switch to respond.

I pressed the button again and
overheard a tour guide answer
questions from schoolchildren
about growing up as a Chinese
in the 60s. The words
on the exhibit lit up briefly
but before I could look again
the bulb which had illuminated
the entire room finally expired.

Guangdong sidewalk

It's time to savour your European life. At the airport
she combs her hair back into the Third World War:

Style is effortless the same way it's easy
to have something unless everyone wants it too.

What emerges from urban pixellation is the greyest
of mysteries, furtive glance down an original side street.

You take each such image & let it vibrate
beneath the weight of two dialects, a single script.

I would join the chorus, though here
we pass only as much as one remains.

Soon the administrator's garden, meandering,
revelation in the updraught of a smog-free sky.

Unfolding

May 2008 – Chengdu, Sichuan, China

A private celebration: mother
weeps; string of cameras carries
this likeness to row upon row of the remote.
What can you feel when the day turns to stone?

On a white beach south-west of Santiago
they feel it too: goose bumps in the cool sea breeze;
frosted glasses of Piña Colada; space afloat,
emptied. Handfuls of silence that pock-mark the air.

Then the unfolding of tides, lightly creased
linen of a surface which entombs
such reactions: nameless black water
layer upon layer of the stuff.

Skimming back across oceans to where a coordinated
wail rings out, appeasing humiliation
with pronouns & possessives
igniting public squares & campuses,
propane fists, their uranium hearts:
emotions when definite become
sharp, cut through whole crowds. This atonement
for the reckless anarchy of earth.

Against a sunset human shadows are
as paper dolls, barbs of phosphorescent light.
Finally, the arrival of the dead in wave
upon wave of photographs, spliced
narratives: unfurling,
an open wound, its destructive pomp.

Immortal

Dim sum, the city's great tradition: the captain of the steam cart
makes a beeline for our table across the vulgar carpet,
then zigzags port-side at the last minute.

We hide our disappointment behind credit cards:
what *can't* you find in a supermarket these days!?
In Aisle 4: plantation palm oil & the latest flavonoids.
Aisle 6: this numinous stream of crockery & chopsticks.

Ours was a world less innocent than such winding threads
of fluoro strip lights & the gradual advent of disposable nappies.

For old times sake, let's label our prejudices for the sample jars.
We'll examine them tomorrow, over an ice-cold mango drink,
in the laced shade of these hat brims,
though such a taxonomy is sure to kill the mood.

Today remains your day. From his shrine, the North God
delegates aesthetic decisions as to the appearance of his idols –
that old fraudster! When the whistle blows, migrant workers
swim beneath the bridge and back to their dormitories,
a procession of orange hard-hats and flip-flops.

If you have every seen such a sight
you are either immortal or a liar – for only now,
in the fragrant patio of dusk, do a pride of rosewood lions
pad out from the razed mangroves & prowl the foreshore
pawing at a rattan ball marked *Made in Burma.*

the white horse

Wanting so much to learn the classifier for poems
about classifiers, I sought out the wisest teacher;
she handed me a black ceramic pot the spout of which
now daily flowers into smog. I needed more:
the Second Way, she said, was a devotion
to propaganda, perhaps a shot at life on the petulant seas.
But the white stallion with its cloud-draped hooves
& silk-thread mane never turned up for collection.
Nor did my Vietnamese mother who had forsaken me on this,
the eve of the lunar new year. Only thus did I learn
that I am from Australia, that I am an Australian
– an ungracious people, I have read, whose marketable skills
include pressing the eject button on history,
that constellation of CD players in the sky.
& so I was: a spinning disc who spoke often

but recorded nothing, not even the tiniest byte.
I had a thirst that strong white liquor couldn't quench.
I was always hungry, especially at night.
For hours I would channel surf a TV that had been turned
upside down & emptied of intelligible signs.
Once I woke up parched in the first gradient of day
when the morning meal is not yet served;
the eggs, alive & cackling. In empty
rooms throughout the hotel, lacy curtains heaved out
– absolute silence – snatching at grey, smoke-laden air.

After Wang Lü

I tip my hat to those Ming court artists,
each one noted for their meticulous paintings
of bright birds & propitious flowers:
precise black strokes, exact pigment for feather
& petal, bringing close the day. On the sidelines
of such style I screw up the latest draft & it floats
out the window where the sharp crags of Hua Shan &
Mount Druitt's forlorn retail strip are framed.
Sunset's corona burns up the bald horizon; migrating
Learjets & helicopters exchange vicious blows,
divvying up the oil. It's a triage of sweetness,
sadly necessary in these times of short supply.

As in all landscapes there is a human figure
for scale. Whether it be me or you is not important,
nor that here the figure is in plain view,
free at last from the picture's interminable mists:
you pack a reed basket with the paper folio
a third party has chosen to outlive us, & make
for the denuded hills; I push my shopping trolley
across the pot-holed bitumen towards the car.

Now is the time to deliver our best lines to the viewer
though this assumes we can be heard above the explosions
& the lumbering contraption which stomps out
from the gallery shadows; the slight scroll hung
carefully on the wall doesn't stand a chance.

Translucent Jade

My grandfather made me a gift when I was born.
I used it for a while until another gift, my mother's,
flashed in view. Common in its place of origin, here
her gift sparkled and sang, replaced the other.
Not that his was jostled aside, but it sort of slipped away.
No one seemed to mind, if they noticed, as it lay in disuse
and then was quite forgotten.

Today I retrieved his gift from its silence.
Barely, rarely used, it seemed mostly new.
Pristine. I tried it on.
It was a little strange,
as if from a world I hadn't inhabited but had heard stories about.
Sometimes I felt an imposter.
Sometimes I thought it reflected hidden aspects I could own.

What vibrations are these?
Does this begin to become me,
do I to it belong?
This translucent, slowly-yielding music
Chinese name.

Front Page Photo

With a calculated jokey carelessness
the smiling uniformed personnel
let trim snarly dogs jerk and snap
at the genitals of the naked man.
Tell me which is the terrorist.

Andantino

A message of love...Pope Benedict reaches out of his popemobile to kiss an infant as he arrives at Randwick racecourse to celebrate Mass in front of more than 300,000 pilgrims. During his homily he warned of the spread of a "spiritual desert".
— Photo caption *SMH* 21ˢᵗJuly 2008

Was I not sufficient
that you had to gather me up
in an unholy dash to join 350,000;
that you had to have me
pushed determinedly higher and higher
by a black-suited man unbeknownst to me,
bandied above the surging one-mouthed multitude
(orange knapsack extravaganza),
confused, my legs dangling
~ the helicopter's splitting urgency ~
lifted heavenwards
toward the caped capped elderly pontiff
protruding purposefully from the augmented car
~ window electronically wound open ~
who clasps me about the head,
kisses me on the diamond fontanelle?
Did you think that only then I would be whole?

Did you not see
that I had already arrived
and the assuredness, the eloquence of my vehicle
~ no concocted bubble ~
the word made flesh
beyond voluptuous seeded sweetness of figs;
miracle reflecting sunshine
here unentombed;
supple, fresh of limb, echoing stars
the flesh andantino

clear of desert, unburdened, gift of the gods (and to them):
your offspring?
Did my self
not enchant, awaken, focus, my father?
You were still awaiting
confirmation at an appointed hour
from some other's ringed hands and homily.

The Sprig

The man in the photo is a green shoot of a man
a slim-waisted sprig
a pocket-watch spring
with ears like the wings of a jumbo jet.
He'll take off and you better catch on.

The shades of white and grey can't hide
his technicolour visions.
Through the creased paper protrudes
a jaunty ambition swelling by the second.

I think his rakish moustache just sprouted another hair.

I know how he'll unfurl.
He will build empires.
He will populate the earth.
He will feed multitudes.
He will shower the land with dollar bills.
Then: a modest monument, a humble knighthood,
a self-commissioned portrait hanging in the hallway.

But let's keep this a secret
or he'll never get over himself.

The Baby Biter

My grandfather is a gluttonous man.
A wide-bottomed belly and a set of false teeth.
He indulges in curry puffs in his twilight years,
and plenty of condensed milk
in his tea, and—though it always ends in tears—
he is fond of biting babies.

To express his delight for darling babies
(he means no harm), this dear old man,
braving the warm saltwater of tears,
grabs a chubby arm and sinks his teeth
into the flesh as white as milk
into the meat of fresh born years.

To the life thickened with these years
who can deny the joy of babies,
grown fat sucking mother's milk?
The birthright of a sweet old man
is his sweet grandchild, whose budding teeth
draws out a mother's tears.

The mother laughs, wipes the tears
away. Our family sits—as they have for years—
talking, tearing at curry puffs with our teeth,
grinning lovingly at our dearest babies,
promising when they're full-grown women and men
the sun and the moon and flowing milk

and honey will be theirs. Sweet sweet milk
and thick thick honey. So hush, no tears.
They are lulled by the clinking of china. The old man
leans back, surveys the fruits of his years and years
of living, sitting at this table: his precious babies
for whom he feels again an ache in his teeth.

And he smiles, displaying his perfect teeth,
asks a grandson to pass the condensed milk
his way—one consolation in a life full of babies
of tears
of years
cloying to a man.

A baby's sweet tears
and a mother's rich milk
only tickle the jaws of an old man.

The Steel Trap

The old man's wrath spills out
in stops and starts.
Dribbles out like the pee
his bladder can no longer hold in,
pitter spattering all over the tiles and carpet
his daughters recently installed to
cushion the blow
if he falls.
again.

All time is pyjama time.
But no time is sleeping time
because all hours are edged with anger;
because old anger grows sharper with age
and never grows to a point
like how, now a day never grows into night
and the nights are the same as the days
and there were never seasons on the equator
so he can't (could never, maybe) keep track.

Oh but he can.
All too well.

Maybe not with numbers,
the sums he had an aptitude for,
still has, he insists—
the glistening steel trap mind that
has made him what he is today:

A Big Businessman,
Tycoon Extraordinaire
with a memory for the numbers
for the buying and the selling.
You have to have
a mind for the numbers.

He keeps track
with the empty places around the dining table and
the great basin of winter melon soup and
three different types of stir-fried vegetables and
the watermelon, the durian, the pomelo,
the whole steamed grouper and the chicken curry and
the jar of pineapple tarts that reads
Happy Chinese New Year from
someone or other
given either last year or this one,
so much food that it appears
and reappears for weeks
for years
for days
for all meals.

He keeps track
with the endless rooms lacking
fortresses made of sheets and cushions and
overturned rosewood chairs and stools,
two generations of ringing giggles and toys and messes
and soft little lips of whom he could demand
a kiss on the cheek and who make a pout
because his moustache is too scratchy
and nonetheless comply with his wishes.

He keeps track
with the acid that spurts

from his lips because it hurts too much
to contain himself;
that severs his flesh and blood
from his flesh and blood and
slices the tears from their eyes
in old familiar words that sting, stang, stung:
Lousy.
Ungrateful.
Useless.
Ungrateful.

But all times are pyjama time
And now is the day, like all hours, to sleep
to slumber, to rest, to wait, to stare
ceaselessly into the void of a moonlit ceiling
and count the days, minutes, decades, seconds
until death
or revenge
because they will be the same thing,
mark his words.

House

The walls tremor with a private language –
carving a sound sculpture of a musical elegy,
like a requiem for her sleepless soul.

Unafraid,
she brings herself to a curtailing ostinato,
breathing, soaking as self-pitying woe.

The city abode confines her with
a strange solitude,
she is yearning for something
like dispersion.
Her extinguished eyes
gaze at invisible dust.

Feet crawl on broken pavements
obedient in structure and anatomy –
they pace with diligent trust in a heavy head, though–
they should beware
of a head too fruitful
for small talk
    and
hollow prayers.

They settle with a blur,
accepting the inevitable –

tomorrow will rise like today,
a repetition of yesterday.

My mother's heart is a small, good thing

My mother's heart is a small, good thing.
It is lovely and unassuming like my stain glassed mosaic lamp
illuminating a room as an angel lights the skies.
It is calm like the winds on a gentle Sunday at three.
It hums quietly to itself when no one is listening.
It never stirs at the absence of peace.

My mother's heart is a small, good thing.
It sings at the sight of a neighbour's garden
transforms her willowy feature to delicate soft expressions,
her heart is a keen student.
It swallows with the force of a sea cave, it
kills all light.
Her inevitable freedom, uncaged -
Her fear is mightier than might.
She hums to her own tuneful language,
her solid stare, unpardonable —
she leaks through me like a bleeding creature
her agility fails tonight,
and I have nothing but my intermediate embrace
to comfort.
To comfort.

The Fish Market

The taste of the quiet air
unmoved this morning in the drawing rays of sunlight.
The sea has abandoned these gilled creatures.

In her restlessness, it has been done.

She stands beside me weeping,
fish of the sea,
thrust out of her mighty arms – the reek of injustice.

Abandoned to the cruelty
the diligent indifference of nature –
out of the womb, it withers
a lost meek of sounds too shallow for ears.

She stands beside me like a first aid kit –
her whispers arrive by my side unclothed.
I say with unpardonable angst
your skin is washed with self pity,
your love swells hearts and hollows minds.

She said she felt like a foreigner
in her own country
an asylum seeker on the streets she grew up –
a face too keen to diminish.

This terrifying freedom is swirling between my childish hands.
I look to you for instruction,
tell me what to do
tell me who to love.
I go today to be pounded by the sea,
like the fish that is destined here in the city's dawn.

The Fish Market Before

Twirling scents
defrost the dawn air.
The reek of frozen hard flesh,
the pungent assault on our senses,
delivers little solace to our daughter
as she cradles your fingers in her
gentle sleep.
This morning -
the fish are swirling in their dead bodies -
a generation of water creatures,
I ask, 'Did they know this was going to be their grave?'
Did you know, you were
to return here to these streets?
A hand rests on top of the silver railings,
a severed heart swells deep inside its anchor.
On this ancient land, your soul seems to wither,
in the deep, confusion you now have -
you cry because you are now a foreigner in your own land.
'I am an asylum seeker, here – where I used to live.
My mother and father raised me here with crippling hands and
                                        uncooked rice,
I am the alien, they've come to despise.'

Acknowledgements and Permissions

Every effort has been made to acknowledge the ownership and use of copyrighted material. The editors regret any errors or omissions, which will be corrected if there should be a subsequent edition.

Adam Aitken, 'Changi' and 'Alexandria' from *Romeo and Juliet in Subtitles*, Brandl and Schlesinger (2006); 'A Biography of 13', 'For Effendi, Emperor of Icecream', 'Aubade 1', 'Aubade 2' and 'The Wearer of Amulets' from *Eighth Habitation*, Giramondo (2009). Ivy Alvarez, 'there's only ever been two' in *Cordite* (2005), 'En las montañas' and 'The Pastoralist Speaks' in *Cordite* (2008), and 'Curing the animal' in *Best Australian Poems*, Black Inc. Publishing (2010), and *Prairie Schooner* (2012). Mona Zahra Attamimi, 'In the Year of the Dragon', 'The Last Drop', 'The Jewel of Java', 'The 1740 Massacre of Chinese Immigrants in Batavia (old Jakarta)' courtesy of the author. Desh Balasubramaniam, 'The zoo' and 'My country, my lover' in *Mascara Literary Review 9*; 'Waiting for freedom' in *Mascara Literary Review 9*; 'Smoke Of Zebu' in *Trout*, December 2010, Volume 16 (Aotearoa/New Zealand). Merlinda Bobis 'This is where it begins' from *Asian Australia & Asian America: Making Transnational Connections*. Special issue of *Amerasia Journal* 36.2 (2010) 151-152.; 'Driving to Katoomba' and 'Siesta' from *Summer Was A Fast Train Without Terminals*, Spinifex Press (1998); 'Covenant' and 'Litany' from *Pag-uli, Pag-uwi, Homecoming. Poetry in Three Tongues*. University of Santo Tomas Publishing House, Manila, (2004). *Covenant*, adapted sound drama by Australian Broadcasting Corporation ABC Radio. Kim Cheng Boey, 'La Mian in Melbourne' and 'Plum Blossom or Quong Tart at the QVB' from *After the Fire*, Firstfruits (2006); 'Stamp-collecting' and 'Clear Brightness' from *Clear Brightness*, Epigram/Puncher & Wattmann (2012). Michelle Cahill, 'Kālī from Abroad', 'Pārvatī in Darlinghurst' and 'Ode to Mumbai,' from *Vishvarūpa*, Five Islands Press (2011); 'Swans' in *Night Birds*, Vagabond Press (2012); 'Day of a Seal, 1820' in *Cordite* 41.0. Andrew Carruthers, 'Love's Legend, a Sermon,' 'reading Mao in the future', and 'Hong Kong, 1999' courtesy of the author. Carol Chan, 'Learning to Leave' and 'Miles' in *Softblow*, June (2010); 'Popcorn' and 'Common State' in *The World Must Weigh the Same*, Math Paper Press (2011); 'Away', 'On Seeing A "Uniquely Singapore" Advertisement in Australian *Vogue*' courtesy of the author. Ken Chau, 'Chinese Silence No. 101' and 'Chinese Silence No. 103' in *Mascara Literary Review*, 13; 'Chinese Silence No. 102', 'Chinese Silence No. 104', and 'Chinese Silence No. 105' courtesy of the author. Eileen Chong, 'My Hakka Grandmother', 'Lu Xun, your hands', 'Mid-Autumn Mooncakes', 'Winter Meeting', 'Grandmother's Dish' and 'Lu Xun's Wife', from

Burning Rice, Australian Poetry New Voices Series 2012, Melbourne. Christopher Cyrill, 'Extracts from *Quaternion – a prose poem novella'* in *Heat 24*, 2011. Paul Dawson, 'Possible Worlds' in *Australian Poetry Journal* 1.1 (2011); 'Sydney', and excerpt from 'Thanks for all the poems Pauline Hanson' from *Imagining Winter* (Interactive Press, 2006), 'Reading Hopkins', 'Dickinson's Envelope' courtesy of the author. Ee Tiang Hong, 'Done', 'Resolution', 'Requiem', 'Perth', 'Some New Perspectives', from *Nearing a Horizon* (UniPress 1994); 'For My Son' from *Myths for a Wilderness*, Heinemann Asia (1976). Sunil Govinnage, 'On Becoming an Intellectual', 'White Mask', 'Summer in Perth', 'Fremantle Beach' and 'Pettah Market' from *White Mask*, iUniverse, (2003). Louise Ho, 'A Veteran Talking', 'Incense Tree, Aquilaria Sinensis', 'Party', and 'The Other Day' from *Incense Tree: Collected Poems of Louise Ho*, Hong Kong University Press, (2009). Subhash Jaireth, 'The Rains (1, 2, 3, 5, 6)' and 'The Empty Table' from *Unfinished Poems for Your Violin*, Penguin Australia (1996); 'The Empty Table', 'Autumn (3)' and 'Winter (5)' from *Yashodhara: Six Seasons without You*, Wild Peony (2003); 'Meena, the Elephant, in the Kabul Zoo' in *Thylazine: Poets for Peace* (2003). Bella Li, 'E 44 10 N 33 15' and 'Voyage' in *Mascara Literary Review 10* (2011); 'South of the water' and 'Two children are threatened by a, 1924' in *Otoliths Issue 21* (2011); 'Drowning dream' and 'Winter' courtesy of the author. Debbie Lim, 'How to Grow Feet of Golden Lotus' in *Mascara Literary Review* 4 (2008); 'Whale', 'The Vampire Squid' and 'Bodies of Pompeii' in *Beastly Eye*, Vagabond Press, (2012); 'Thoughts of Bamboo' in *Blue Dog* Vol 6 No 12 (2008); 'Meeting the Owl' in *Magma* (UK), Issue 52 (2011). Miriam Wei Wei Lo, 'Home' and 'Mooncake' in *Poetry Without Borders*, Picaro Press (2008); 'Bumboat Cruise on the Singapore River', 'Like the Autumn Clouds, They are Gone' from *Against Certain Capture*, Five Islands Press (2004). Gita Mammen, 'Recycled' from *Feefafafaluda*, Five Islands Press (2006); 'Prophet on Flinders' in *Etchings*, Vol 6, (2009); 'Ghazal to a Qana child', 'Night Kitchen' and 'Tiger Nights' courtesy of the author. Sudesh Mishra, 'Elegy: Ee Tiang Hong', 'A Tropical Babu' *Tandava*, Meanjin Press, Melbourne (1992); 'A Bilimbili for Madelaine' in *Diaspora and the Difficult Art of Dying*, University of Otago Press, Dunedin, New Zealand (2002). 'About Aji', 'A Wishing Well in Suva' and 'Dowry' courtesy of the author. Omar Musa, 'Gran/Nenek', 'Airforce Ones' and 'Queanbeyan' from *The Clocks*, Muse Arts Magazine (2009); 'Lightning Over Sandakan', 'A Homeland' and 'Felda' from *Parang*, Blast! Publishing (2013). Nguyễn Tiên Hoàng, 'Thursday April 21. Canberra', 'For St Kilda Road', 'They' and 'Elegy' from *Years, Elegy*, Vagabond Press (2012); 'Travel' in *Poetryinternationalweb* (2012). Ouyang Yu, 'Fragments of an Evening Walk in Kingsbury' and 'Spring Festival' from *Foreign Matter* (2003); 'Writing a poem, in the sun' and 'New Accents' from *The Kingsbury Tales*, Brandl & Schlesinger (2008); 'The Double Man' and 'An Identity CV' from *New and Selected Poems*, Salt (2004). Suneeta Peres da Costa, 'The Changed Woman' and 'The Mirror Man' in *Mascara Literary Review*10; 'The Wounded Butcher', 'Crossroads', 'Oriental Lilies' and 'Healing' courtesy of the author. Vuong Pham, 'Mother' and 'Father' from *Refugee Prayer*, Brisbane New Voices (2013); 'Fall of Saigon' in *Peril* 14; 'Refugee Prayer' in *Sampad* (Tagore Writing Competition, 2012). Andy Quan, 'Quiet and Odd' from *Bowling Pin Fire*, Signature Editions (2007); 'Mr. Wong's Children', 'Resonance', 'The Leg Crosser' from *Slant*, Nightwood Editions (Canada, 2001); 'Is this?' in *Poetry International Web* (2009). Adam Raffel, 'Ranjith Singh's School Days', 'The Kadalay Woman' and 'Immigration Blues' courtesy of the author. Christine Ratnasingham, 'The Foreigner' and 'Dark skin' in *Mascara Literary Review* 12 (2012); 'Ghosts' and 'Periwinkle blue' courtesy of the author. Jaya Savige, 'Currency Lad' and 'Mandarin' from *Latecomers*, UQP (2005); 'Arrowtown', 'Recycling Night', 'Missile' and 'Circular Breathing' from *Surface to Air*, UQP (2011). Shen, 'Today', 'Noodles', 'Geography', *'from* Ancestral Shadows', and 'Highlights' from *City of My Skin*, Five Islands Press (2001). James Stuart, 'Guangdong sidewalk' in *Mascara Literary Review* 7 (2010); 'Unfolding' and 'Immortal' from *Imitation Era*, Vagabond Press (2012); 'the white horse' courtesy of the author; 'After Wang Lü' in *Heat 20* (2009). Maureen Ten (Ten Ch'in Ü), 'Translucent Jade' in International Chinese Language Forum (2013); 'Front Page Photo' and 'Andantino' courtesy of the author. Tiffany Tsao, 'The Sprig' in *Mascara Literary Review* 12 (2012), 'The Baby Biter' and 'The Steel Trap' courtesy of the author. Jessie Tu, 'House', 'My mother's heart is a small, good thing' in *Mascara Literary Review* 11 (2012); 'The Fish Market' and 'The Fish Market Before' courtesy of the author.

Biographies

ADAM AITKEN was born in London and spent his early childhood in Malaysia and Thailand, before his family settled in Sydney. His writing has been widely anthologised, and his most recent collections include *Eighth Habitation* (Giramondo), *Tonto's Revenge* (Tinfish Press, Hawai'i), *The Bats of Angkor Wat* (Picaro Press), and *November Already* (Vagabond Press). In 2011-12 he was resident at the Australia Council's Keesing Studio, Paris, and in Southern France, completing new poems and a memoir. He teaches creative writing at the University of Technology, Sydney.

IVY ALVAREZ is the author of *Mortal* (2006), and *Disturbance* (Seren Books, 2013), written with support from the Australia Council and from Literature Wales. Her poems feature in anthologies (including *Best Australian Poems 2009*), journals and new media in many countries and online, with several translated into Russian, Spanish, Japanese and Korean. She held both the MacDowell and Hawthornden Fellowships in 2005. Born in the Philippines and raised in Australia, she has lived in Wales, UK since 2004.

MONA ZAHRA ATTAMIMI is Arab Indonesian. She lived in Asia and North America before settling in Sydney at age nine. She has a Masters of Letters in Creative Writing from the University of Sydney. Her poems have appeared in *Meanjin, Southerly and Mascara Literary Review.*

DESH BALASUBRAMANIAM is a young poet. He was born in Sri Lanka and raised in both the war-torn Northern & Eastern provinces. At the age of thirteen, he fled to New Zealand with his family on humanitarian asylum. During and upon conclusion of his University education, he travelled on shoestring budgets through a number of countries, hitchhiking and working various jobs. His continuous journeys have evoked his passion for expressive art and launched him on the endless quest for identity. He is the founding director of Ondru – a movement of arts & literature (www.ondru.org). His poetical work has appeared in *Overland, Going Down Swinging, the Lumière Reader, Mascara Literary Review, Blackmail Press, Trout, QLRS, the Typewriter, Cha: An Asian Literary Journal* and other publications. He is currently working on his first poetry collection.

MERLINDA BOBIS is a Filipino-Australian writer and performer who has published in three languages across multiple genres. Her novels, short story and poetry books, and plays have received various awards, including the Prix Italia, the

Steele Rudd Award for the Best Published Collection of Australian Short Stories, the Philippine National Book Award, and the Australian Writers' Guild Award. She has been short-listed for *The Age* Poetry Book Award and the Australian Literature Society Gold Medal. She has performed her dramatic works in Australia, Philippines, US, Canada, Spain, France, and China. Her latest novel is *Fish-Hair Woman*. She teaches Creative Writing at the University of Wollongong.

KIM CHENG BOEY was born in Singapore in 1965 and migrated to Australia in 1997. He has published five collections of poetry and a travel memoir entitled *Between Stations*. He teaches Creative Writing at the University of Newcastle.

MICHELLE CAHILL is a Goan-Anglo-Indian writer who was born in Kenya, lived in the UK and resides in Sydney. She writes poetry, fiction and essays, and edits *Mascara Literary Review*. Her awards include the Val Vallis Award, the Inverawe Prize (minor), the VPLA shortlist and a highly commended in the Blake Poetry Prize. She was a fellow at Hawthornden Castle and Sanskriti Kendra Retreat, New Delhi. She has received an International Writing Fellowship at Kingston University, London in 2013.

ANDREW CARRUTHERS was born in Auburn, Sydney in 1987. His mother was born in Hong Kong and migrated to Australia in her late teens to study at Marrickville Public School before being offered a university place in the Whitlam years. Raised and educated in Sydney, Andrew writes on musical analogy, musical notation and militant politics in 20th Century long poems.

CAROL CHAN was born in Singapore. Her writing has been published in *Cordite Poetry Review, Wet Ink, Meanjin, Softblow Poetry Journal, Quarterly Literary Review Singapore, Ceriph,* and *The Lilliput Review.* She is also the editorial assistant for *Mascara Literary Review,* and author of *The World Must Weigh the Same* (chapbook, Math Paper Press 2011). She is currently a graduate student in Anthropology, following stories of mobility and stasis between Indonesia, Singapore, and other lands.

KEN CHAU is a poet living in Melbourne, Australia. His poems have been published in Australia, France, Hong Kong, India, UK and USA.

EILEEN CHONG is a Sydney poet who was born in Singapore. In 2010 she won the Poets Union Youth Fellowship. Her first collection, *Burning Rice*, was published in 2012 by Australian Poetry.

CHRISTOPHER CYRILL is the author of two novels, *The Ganges and Its Tributaries* (Penguin, 1993) and *Hymns for the Drowning* (Allen & Unwin, 1999). He is currently working on his third novel *Quarternion*. He is also a short story writer, playwright and poet. He began publishing his work in 1987 and served for many years as the fiction editor for *HEAT* magazine and the fiction editor of Giramondo Publishing. He has taught creative writing at various universities for over twelve years. His work has appeared in hundreds of Australian and international journals and magazines. He is currently completing a Doctorate in Creative Arts at the University of Sydney and managing his small editing/ mentoring business The Collected Fiction.

PAUL DAWSON'S book of poems, *Imagining Winter* (Interactive Press, 2006), won the national IP Picks Best Poetry Award in 2006, and his poetry has been anthologised in *Harbour City Poems: Sydney in Verse 1788-2008* (Puncher & Wattmann, 2009). Paul's poetry and short fiction have appeared in a range of literary journals and newspapers, including: Meanjin, Island, Southerly, Overland, Snorkel, Slope (US), The Sleeper's Almanac, Australian Poetry Journal, Blue Dog: Australian Poetry, Imago: New Writing, and The Sydney Morning Herald. He is also the author of *Creative Writing and the New Humanities* (Routledge, 2005) and *Twenty-first Century Omniscience: Authorship and Narrative Authority in the New Millennium* (forthcoming with the Ohio State University Press). Paul is a Senior Lecturer in the School of Arts and Media at the University of New South Wales where he teaches Creative Writing and literary studies.

EE TIANG HONG was born in Malacca in 1933, a seventh-generation Baba or Straits-born Chinese, a descendent of intermarriage between the Malays and Chinese. Ee was unhappy with political developments that promoted Malay ascendancy since Malaysia's independence. Dismayed by the dark day in Malaysian history, May 13th 1969, when racial riots broke out in Kuala Lumpur and nearly 200 people were killed, and disenchanted by the policies that ensued, Ee emigrated to Australia in 1975, settling in Guildford, Perth. He died of cancer in April 1990. Ee is one of the pioneering South-East Asian poets who chose to write in English, the colonial language, but made it his own so that it embraced local accents and reflected the realities of the post-colonial landscape. His collections include *Tranquerah, Myths for a Wilderness* and the posthumously published *Nearing a Horizon*.

SUNIL GOVINNAGE has been writing poetry in Sinhala since 1965, and in English since 1989. He has published numerous poems in journals and newspapers in Sri

Lanka, Australia and the USA. Some of his works have also been broadcast on radio in Sri Lanka and Singapore. In 1998, Govinnage read some of his poetry at the Eleventh Commonwealth Triennial Conference on Literature and Language, held in Kuala Lumpur, along with distinguished poets from Commonwealth countries. His books include: *White Mask*, (iUniverse, 2003) and *Perth: My Village Down Under* (Sarasavi Publishers, 2011).

LOUISE HO emigrated from Hong Kong to Australia in 1994, took Australian citizenship in 1996 and has finally settled here since 2003. Since the 70s her poetry has appeared in international journals, anthologies and books. She retired from the Chinese University of Hong Kong where she lectured on English/American Poetry and Shakespeare. Her collected poems *Incense Tree* was published by Hong Kong University Press in 2009.

SUBHASH JAIRETH was born in India. Between 1969 and 1978 he spent nine years in Moscow. In 1986 he came to Canberra. He has published poetry, fiction and non-fiction in Hindi, Russian and English.

MISBAH KHOKHAR is a poet and musician who was born in Pakistan. Her time is mostly occupied in making things; music and poetry that are concerned with the themes of identity, memory, and imagined spaces. She completed her MPhil in Poetry at U.Q and her manuscript 'Rooftops in Karachi' went on to be highly commended in 2010, 2011, and 2012 Thomas Shapcott Poetry Prize. Her poetry has been published in the *Australian Poetry Journal, Cordite,* and *Mascara Literary Review.* She has been performing both as a musician and a poet since her early 20's singularly, and in collaboration with other musicians and artists. She is currently working on more poetry to form part of a collection she is calling 'Animal Kingdom', a natural follow on from 'Rooftops in Karachi'. She currently lives, writes and performs in Melbourne.

BELLA LI is a Melbourne poet. Born in China, she immigrated to Australia with her parents at the age of three. Since graduating with a double degree in arts and law from the University of Melbourne, she has worked as a research assistant, judge's associate, proofreader and editor. Her poems have been published in journals including *Meanjin, Cordite, Otoliths* and *Mascara Literary Review,* and anthologised in the *Paradise Poetry Anthology* and *Best Australian Poems 2012.* A chapbook of her work will be published by Vagabond Press, as part of the limited edition Rare Objects Series, in late 2013.

DEBBIE LIM was born in Sydney. Her maternal grandfather migrated from Zhejiang Province, China, to the Philippines in the 1920s. Her awards include the Rosemary Dobson Prize (2009), Dorothy Sargent Rosenberg Prizes (2008, 2010) and the Inverawe Nature Poetry Prize (2008, 2010). A chapbook, *Beastly Eye*, was published by Vagabond Press in 2012. She is working towards a first full-length collection.

MIRIAM WEI WEI LO is more certain than ever as she approaches forty that what she wants out of art is meaning and beauty. Her previous work includes *Against Certain Capture* (which won the 2005 WA Premier's Prize) and *No Pretty Words* (Picaro Press, 2010). She lives in Margaret River with her family.

GITA MAMMEN is a Melbourne based writer and visual artist who often combines the two art forms in projects. *Feefafafaluda*, her collection of poetry, was published by Five Islands Press, New Poets Series 11. *Lode rust*, her artist-book of poetry and etchings is held by Rare Books, State Library of Victoria, and Special Collections, National Library, Canberra.

SUDESH MISHRA was born in Suva and educated in Fiji and Australia. He has been the recipient of an ARC Postdoctoral Fellowship, the Harri Jones Memorial Prize for Poetry and an Asialink Residency. He is the author of four books of poems, including *Tandava* (Meanjin Press) and *Diaspora and the Difficult Art of Dying* (Otago UP), two critical monographs, *Preparing Faces: Modernism and Indian Poetry in English* (Flinders University and University of the South Pacific) and *Diaspora Criticism* (Edinburgh UP), two plays *Ferringhi* and *The International Dateline* (Institute of Pacific Studies, Suva), and several short stories. Sudesh has also co-edited *Trapped*, an anthology of writing from Fiji. His creative work has appeared in a wide array of publications, including *Nuanua: Pacific Writing in English since 1980*, *The Indigo Book of Modern Australian Sonnets*, *Lines Review: Twelve Modern Young Indian Poets*, *Over There: Poems from Singapore and Australia*, *Sixty Indian Poets*, *The Bloodaxe Book of Contemporary Indian Poetry*, *The HarperCollins Book of English Poetry*, *The World Record* and *Concert of Voices: An Anthology of World Writing in English*. Sudesh is working on a fifth collection of poems, a collaborative project on popular Hindi cinema (with Vijay Mishra) and a series of papers on minor history. He is currently Professor in Literature, Language and Linguistics at the University of the South Pacific.

OMAR MUSA is a Malaysian-Australian rapper and poet from Queanbeyan, Australia. He is a winner of the Australian Poetry Slam and the Indian Ocean Poetry Slam. He has released three hip hop albums and two collections of poetry, *The Clocks* and *Parang* (2013). He is part of international hip hop group MoneyKat and his debut novel *Here Come the Dogs* will be published by Penguin Australia in 2014.

Nguyễn Tiên Hoàng arrived in Australia from Vietnam in 1974 under a Colombo Plan Scholarship. He graduated from Monash University in Melbourne, worked with Radio Australia and now works in information technology. His poems have appeared in the *Saturday Age*, *HEAT*, and Black Inc Publishing anthologies of *Best Australian Poems*. Under the pen name Thương Quán, his poems and essays in Vietnamese have appeared in various literary journals in Australia, Vietnam, the United States and Europe. His writings can be read on current online literary magazines including damau.org, tienve.org and Poetry International website. His most recent book is *Years, Elegy*, (Vagabond Press, 2012).

Ouyang Yu came to Australia at the age of thirty-five, and has published sixty-nine books in English and Chinese languages, including the award-winning novel *The Eastern Slope Chronicle* (2002), a collection of poetry in English, *The Kingsbury Tales* (2008), a collection of Chinese poetry, *Slow Motion* (2009), and a book of creative non-fiction, *On the Smell of an Oily Rag: Speaking English, Thinking Chinese and Living Australian* (2008). His second novel, *The English Class* (2010), won the Community Relations Commission Award in the 2011 New South Wales Premier's Literary Award, and in the same year was short-listed for the Christina Stead Prize for Fiction, the Western Australia Premier's Awards and the Queensland Premier's Awards. His book of literary criticism is *Chinese in Australian Fiction: 1888-1988* (2008). His translation of Robert Hughes' *The Fatal Shore* is forthcoming in 2013.

Suneeta Peres da Costa was born in Sydney in 1976 to parents of Goan heritage. She is the author of the bestselling novel *Homework* (Bloomsbury), stories, essays and poems in local and international journals and anthologies, as well as numerous dramatic works and feature productions for ABC Radio. She has taught writing over many years at the University of Technology, Sydney, and is currently fiction editor at *Mascara Literary Review*.

Vuong Pham is a Brisbane-based teacher and poet. His poetry has received awards in the *Waterline Writing Competition* (2011); the *Ipswich Poetry Feast Competition* (2012, 2012); the *Inspired by Tagore International Writing Competition* (2012); and the *Free XpresSion Haiku Competition* (2012). His first collection of poems is *Refugee Prayer*, (Brisbane New Voices, 2013). He likes soccer, church, practicing piano, writing and reading poetry, and green tea. His blog is at http://versesoftheinnerself.blogspot.com.au. ANDY QUAN was born in 1969 in Vancouver, B.C., a third-generation Chinese-Canadian and fifth-generation Chinese-American with roots in the villages of Canton. He has lived in Sydney since 1999 and became an Australian citizen in 2006. He is the author of four books. His first collections of poetry, *Slant*, and short fiction, *Calendar Boy*, were released in North America in 2001, the latter was published in Australia by Penguin in 2002 and also nominated for a Lambda Literary Award. In 2005, *Six Positions: Sex Writing by Andy Quan* was published by Green Candy Press. In 2007, his second collection of poetry, *Bowling Pin Fire*, was published through Signature Editions of Winnipeg, Canada. He was also the co-editor of *Swallowing Clouds, an Anthology of Chinese Canadian Poetry*. His website is: www.andyquan.com.

ADAM RAFFEL was born in Colombo, Sri Lanka in 1960 and migrated to Australia with his family in 1975. He is an editor in a large legal publishing company. He has acted in plays and is currently writing his memoirs and working on a novel set in Sydney in the 1980s.

CHRISTINE RATNASINGHAM is a Sydney based writer and poet, who was born in Sri Lanka and grew up in England and Australia. She has had her poetry published in *conversations*, *Extempore*, *Hypallage* and *Mascara Literary Review*, and was awarded the HB Higgins Scholarship for Poetry from the University of Melbourne.

JAYA SAVIGE is the author of *Latecomers* (UQP 2005), which won the NSW Premier's Kenneth Slessor Prize for Poetry, and *Surface to Air* (UQP 2011), which was shortlisted for The Age Poetry Book of the Year. He was born in Sydney in 1978 to an Australian mother and an Indonesian father, and moved with his mum and younger brother to Bribie Island, Queensland, as a young boy after his parents separated. He is currently working on a PhD as a Gates Scholar at the University of Cambridge, Christ's College. He is the Poetry Editor of *The Australian* newspaper.

SHEN has written and had poetry published for sixteen years. His first collection, *City of My Skin*, was published in 2002 by Five Islands Press. He grew up in Malaysia but has lived in Adelaide since 1987. He works full-time as a GP, husband and father of three children.

JAMES STUART'S first collection of poems is *Imitation Era* (Vagabond Press, 2012). His previous work is largely intermedia and includes *Conversions*, an exhibition of poetry in translation (Chengdu, Suzhou and Beijing) and *The Material Poem* (www.nongeneric.net), an e-anthology of text-based art and inter-media writing. He won the 2010 Newcastle Poetry Prize's New Media Category for 'Sudden Rain, Tilba Tilba' a collaboration with artist Laura Gulbin.

MAUREEN TEN (TEN CH'IN Ü) came with her family to Australia from Malaysia 23 years ago. She edited and published *Mood Lightning*, the anthology which won the 2005 Wild & Woolley Prize for poetry. She has performed at the Sydney Writers' Festival with Auburn Poets and Writers Group and is also in a trio, *Running Order*, with Danny Gardner and Bill Tibben. She has convened evenings of poetry and discussion: *Cosmopolitan Sydney in Conversation*.

TIFFANY TSAO grew up in Singapore and Indonesia, has lived in the UK and the United States, and now resides in Sydney, Australia. She holds a doctorate in English from University of Berkeley, California and is a currently a lecturer in English at the University of Newcastle, Australia.

JESSIE TU currently teaches full time at the Rose Bay independent girls school Kambala and enjoys writing as a means of connecting with her community. In 2012, she was awarded a six month residency as a Café Poet (a program funded by the government-assisted Australian Poetry Limited) at her favourite café in Sydney – WellCo Café in Glebe. She has had her writing published in *Peril* and *VibeWire*.

9 781921 450655